NEW YORK POST

Difficult
Su Doku

NEW YORK POST

Difficult
Su Doku

The Official Utterly Addictive
Number-Placing Puzzle

Compiled by Wayne Gould

 **Collins**

An Imprint of HarperCollinsPublishers

First published in Great Britain in 2006 by HarperCollins
Publishers, Ltd.

New York Post © 2006 by NYP Holdings dba New York Post.

HarperCollins books may be purchased for educational, busi-
ness, or sales promotional use. For information please write:
Special Markets Department, HarperCollins Publishers,
10 East 53rd Street, New York, NY 10022.

FIRST U.S. EDITION

ISBN-10: 0-06-117337-1
ISBN-13: 978-0-06-117337-0

06 07 08 09 10   RRD   10 9 8 7

Contents

Introduction

Since its launch in *The Times* in November 2004, Su Doku has become one of the most popular features of the paper and an international phenomenon. In a world where time is apparently a precious commodity, it is a testament to the addictive power of the puzzle that so many people can't wait to tackle it on a daily basis and with such intense concentration. *The Times* books, once they appeared in the bestseller lists, haven't budged since, showing their huge popularity with the book-buying public.

Here is a collection of 200 previously unpublished Difficult Su Doku puzzles from Wayne Gould, the man who started it all. This level is ideal for Su Doku solvers who enjoy the more challenging puzzles. Once mastered, why not give Fiendish a go?

Remember, these puzzles require no guesswork: logic will lead you to a single solution. A valuable tip from Wayne Gould: 'If you are writing too many pencil marks, it means you are not understanding how the puzzle works. You may be relying too much on mechanical procedures, without appreciating the underlying logic. If, in time, you can shake yourself free of written pencil marks, you will see the Su Doku puzzle for what it is – a thing of beauty!'

Puzzles

4			1	5	7	8		
	7	8		3	9		1	6
	1			8	6		7	
9	4	2	3	6	8	1	5	7
7	3	6	9	1	5		8	4
8	5		7	2	4	6	3	9
	8	4	6	7	2	3	9	1
1	2	9	5	4	3	7	2	8
		7	8	9	1	4	6	5

Difficult

			8	1		4		
				9	3	8	2	
							6	7
4	7							8
	9	5				2	7	
1							9	5
8	6							
	5	9	3	2				
		4		8	5			

Su Doku

4	3	5	1	9	6	2	8	7
8	1	9	7	5	2	3	6	4
7	6	2	8	3	4	1	9	5
9	2	1	6	4	8	5	7	3
6	4	7	5	2	3	8	1	9
3	5	8	9	7	1	6	4	2
2	9	6	3	8	7	4	5	1
1	7	3	4	6	5	9	2	8
5	8	4	2	1	9	7	3	6

Difficult

8		1				5		4
	7		9	8	2		3	
1			3		6			2
		3		7		9		
2			5		8			1
	6		4	2	5		1	
9		4				2		3

Su Doku

9	7	2	3	5	6	4	1	8
4	5	3	2	8	1	9	7	6
6	8	1	9	4	7	2	5	3
3	2	6	8	9	5	1	4	7
1	4	7	6	2	3	8	9	5
8	9	5	7	1	4	3	6	2
5	6	9	4	3	8	7	2	1
2	1	8	5	7	9	6	3	4
7	3	4	1	6	2	5	8	9

3			9					
	9			4				
				5	8	1		
		6			5			7
2		5	8		3	9		4
7			2			3		
		2	7	3				
				2			4	
					4			5

			1					
1		9			6			
2		8		9	7		4	
		1	7				8	5
5	3				4	7		
	5		3	8		2		7
			2			9		6
					5			

Difficult

	1			4				
		3	7		2			4
		6				7	1	
	5			7			3	
1			9		3			5
	3			2			7	
	9	5				4		
6			4		7	3		
				9			2	

2				7		1		
				6		9		2
	6		2			4		
					8	5		
5			6		7			3
		8	4					
		6			3		8	
3		1		2				
		5		1				6

Difficult

		5			9		7	
	9		2			6	3	
		1				9		2
	7			4	5			
	8						6	
			8	7			4	
7		9				5		
	3	6			2		1	
	2		1			3		

Su Doku

9				2				5
5		8	1		9	2		4
			8		5			
		6				8		
	2			5			6	
		9				4		
			9		8			
4		7	2		3	5		1
2				7				8

Difficult

		8	3			9	6	
		1	5				7	
9	5						2	
			7		5			9
2			9		4			
	3						8	4
	8				9	7		
	7	5			1	2		

Su Doku

	8						3	
	3		9		6		4	
1		2				8		7
		3	8		4	6		
		8	1		9	4		
2		5				1		8
	9		6		2		7	
	7						5	

Difficult

4								9
						7		3
	3	9		6	4	1	8	
	7		3					
		2	9		8	4		
				6			7	
	6	3	8	1		2	5	
1		4						
5								6

9		4			2			3
			9	3		2		
	3		1					9
1						3	5	
	6						8	
	7	8						6
8					1		6	
		5		7	4			
4			2			5		8

Difficult

	4		2	1			6	
				9	6			
	9					5		
3		6					1	
5			4		8			6
	7					3		2
		9					5	
			1	4				
	2			7	9		4	

	8		1	4				
2			3					
		6		8			3	
6		1				8		
5	4						9	1
		3				6		4
	5			9		1		
					2			9
				6	4		8	

Difficult

9								2
1	3				5		9	
			6	4				
	1			9				4
3		7				8		1
8				3			7	
				7	6			
	7		1				8	9
4								6

				3				9
4				5			2	
5		8			2	3		1
			9				7	8
		5				4		
7	8				1			
2		3	8			6		5
	1			2				4
8				7				

		5				9		
		2				8		
4			8		2			3
	9			7			8	
8			9		6			5
	3			5			7	
6			7		4			2
		7				6		
		3				5		

				3				
2					8	7		
8		3				2		
				8	2		5	7
7				6				8
3	5		9	4				
		9				3		2
		5	4					6
				9				

Difficult

1					6			2
			1		2	4		
	2	4	8			1		
6	8					5	3	
	9	5					2	4
		7			5	8	6	
		8	7		1			
4			3					1

Su Doku

	6							
		9	5	6	1			2
					2		3	
	4	2	8		9		7	
	1						8	
	5		1		3	4	2	
	9		7					
5			9	2	4	8		
							1	

	8			1			6	
		5	7	8	4	1		
		2				4		
5								4
	9		2		3		5	
8								6
		9				8		
		1	8	9	6	5		
	3			4			7	

						9		
2	6			7		5		
				4	3			8
					4	6		3
3			2		7			4
1		6	8					
7			4	5				
		8		9			5	6
		2						

Difficult

	1	3	2					
4	7				1			
		6	3				2	
				3	9	6		
		4				7		
		5	6	4				
	2				3	8		
		9					4	2
					7	1	3	

Su Doku

		1	2		9	7		
		6	1		4	9		
	8						1	
4		7				5		6
	5						7	
3		2				4		9
	7						9	
		5	6		2	3		
		4	3		5	8		

Difficult

	5		1		2		7	
		2	3		7	1		
				9				
7			6		1			8
	4						1	
1			5		4			9
				6				
		6	4		3	2		
	8		9		5		6	

	3		8		5	1		
					3			8
	8	5	4	7				
6						2		3
	5						1	
9		1						7
				1	8	6	7	
7			9					
		6	2		7		4	

Difficult

	1					6		
					5			2
6		3	8		2	7		
	8	9		3		2		
			4		8			
		2		9		3	4	
		5	1		4	8		3
3			6					
		1					7	

Su Doku

3				1	9	8		
1					8	7	9	2
	2							
			2				6	
4			7		3			9
	3			4				
							1	
5	8	7	1					3
		3	4	8				6

Difficult

1					8			7
	3					6	1	
	4		1	2				
6				8		3		
		8	7		9	4		
		5		4				8
				1	7		8	
	9	1					2	
7			4					6

Su Doku

	8			6		7		
6			1					5
			2	7				9
		8			7		4	1
		4				2		
7	1		4			9		
3				5	6			
9					4			3
		2		1			6	

					3		5	
				1	6			
4							8	9
9	3		1			5		8
5								1
6		8			7		2	3
7	9							2
			6	5				
	2		3					

Su Doku

	8				9	1		
						4		
	3				5	9		2
2	6		1					
	4			3			5	
					4		9	6
8		7	3				2	
		3						
		5	8				1	

Difficult

			8			5	3	
						8	7	9
		9	7	2		6		
			5		7			3
	5						6	
3			9		1			
		8		7	4	1		
6	3	5						
	7	4			9			

5	3	9				6	7	
					7		8	5
			2				4	
		7	1					
2			3		9			4
					8	5		
	1				3			
4	2		6					
	9	3				4	1	8

Difficult

9				1	7	5	3	
	5	7			4		2	
			3					8
6								
			1		8			
								4
5				4				
	3		8			2	4	
	4	6	9	7				1

	6		5					
5					1			
2		3		8	6	9		
8		5				7		
			9		3			
		1				6		4
		6	3	7		2		1
			8					9
					4		8	

Difficult

5			8			9		
		8	3			2	5	
9								8
				7	5	4		
	9			8			6	
		5	4	1				
6								4
	4	1			2	6		
		2			7			9

Su Doku

			2	1			8	
5		2	4		3			
					7		6	
	2	7					5	6
9								2
6	5					1	9	
	9		1					
			5		4	9		8
	3			8	6			

	1						7	
		2				9		
		5	3		2	4		
	7			1			4	
1				9				8
	4			8			1	
		7	4		1	2		
		1				5		
	8						9	

		9		2			7	
6	4		3				9	
		7				1		3
				1			5	
9			2		6			1
	1			7				
8		4				5		
	7				9		3	8
	6			8		2		

Difficult

2	4		1	5				
							9	
	7		2			3	1	
				4				9
		3				5		
4				7				
	9	6			1		4	
	8							
				2	5		6	3

		9	6		8	5		
2		5		3		6		4
		1				3		
6			4		3			1
7			1		5			8
		7				8		
5		6		1		4		2
		4	7		6	1		

Difficult

		9	1	2	7	3		
5		1				2		4
2				8				7
	8		3		4		6	
4				5				3
7		3				4		9
		4	7	6	2	1		

Su Doku

		5				6		
		4		9				8
					6	7		3
		2	3				5	
7			1		8			2
	5				7	1		
3		7	9					
2				8		3		
		6				2		

Difficult

			9				5	
		4						6
		2	5					8
	3	5		1				
8	7			6			2	5
				7		8	1	
5					2	9		
3						6		
	6				8			

				4		9	2	
		4					6	7
2			9					1
4	8		6					
			2		4			
				3			8	2
7					1			9
9	2					8		
	1	6		5				

Difficult

	9				3		7	
7						6		2
	5	6				4		
6			8	5	1			
			3		2			
			9	4	7			1
		4				3	1	
3		8						6
	1		2				8	

Su Doku

7				6	5	2		
					9			
4	1				8		9	6
							4	
2		1				8		5
	8							
9	7		1				8	4
			2					
		6	8	4				2

Difficult

	1			5	2	9		
		3		1				8
4			7				3	
9						1		
1	5						9	3
		4						5
	6				1			2
3				7		4		
		7	9	8			1	

		6			2	3		1
1		4				7		
			7			9		
	8		9				1	
				4				
	3				8		5	
		8			3			
		3				8		4
6		5	4			1		

Difficult

	8	9					5	
1		6						9
				9	8		6	4
		5		7				
		4	1		5	9		
				3		5		
3	7		2	1				
9						2		3
	6					7	1	

Su Doku

5			4		1		8	
							1	6
		4		7	9			3
			2	1		8		9
8		9		6	5			
7			5	4		3		
9	3							
	2		1		3			5

					9		4	
3		2		5	6			
			8	7			3	
1	8					5		
	3	4				1	8	
		9					2	4
	1			6	8			
			5	4		3		7
	5		9					

		5	9				2	
7			6	8				
		4		7		3		6
							5	8
	8	9				7	4	
5	2							
4		1		2		9		
				4	7			2
	7				9	5		

Difficult

		8			4	5	2	
7		4		2				
5				7			1	3
9								
	2	7				1	6	
								9
4	5			6				1
				3		6		5
	7	9	2			8		

1	3			8				
		2	4		6		5	
							2	
3						7		
	7	5	9		1	8	4	
		4						3
	8							
	4		6		2	9		
				5			6	4

Difficult

2					7			4
	6		8				3	
3		1		2				
			7	4			8	
			2		9			
	8			5	6			
				1		2		9
	5				8		7	
6			5					3

Su Doku

	3						9	
	7	5		8	9			
4			2		7			6
3			4					
		9				6		
					5			4
7			9		8			1
			3	1		4	2	
	1						8	

		7		3			6	
	8			9				
5	3							
3			9	5		7		
	7	6				2	1	
		1		2	7			8
							5	4
				4			2	
	1			7		8		

5		3						
	2		5	8			7	
						8		2
	3	6	9	4				
			6		7			
				5	8	6	3	
3		7						
	5			2	1		8	
						9		3

Difficult

9								7
	8	2				1	4	
		4	2		8	9		
		3		2		6		
	6						3	
		8		1		7		
		6	7		5	8		
	7	9				3	6	
2								9

Su Doku

	4		6		3	2		
					2			8
3				9	5			
7	6	3						9
		4				5		
9						1	8	6
			2	6				4
2			1					
		9	5		7		6	

Difficult

9					1		5	2
4					8	3		
	6	1				8		
6	9		5		7			
				8				
			3		6		2	7
		6				5	9	
		2	1					6
8	4		7					3

Su Doku

				3	4		2	
				6		7	5	
3		9						
4						1		
1			6		9			5
		3						7
						8		1
	6	8		4				
	4		2	9				

Difficult

			6				9	
8			7			3		
	5	2	9	4		7		
						4	2	9
		9				8		
7	6	4						
		3		9	4	2	1	
		1			6			8
	4				2			

Su Doku

							5	9
4			2				8	6
		1			8			
1				8			7	
	3		5		6		4	
	9			2				1
			4			3		
6	5				1			8
7	4							

			6					
	3	5		1			2	
		2			5	9	8	
		8		7				3
	4		1		2		7	
2				6		1		
	2	3	7			8		
	7			3		4	1	
					1			

Su Doku

	8	7			5			
						6		2
	4		9	2				1
1			3		6	2		
		6				7		
		9	7		2			8
3				1	8		9	
7		4						
			4			3	2	

Difficult

	3	4			5	2		
				1	8			4
8								3
4	1			5				
	5		1		6		4	
			9				5	2
7								9
5			2	8				
		2	6			3	8	

Su Doku

	2		8	3				
				5		6		2
	5	6	4			9		
						4		8
3	7						6	5
2		4						
		8			7	2	3	
7		1		2				
				6	8		5	

Difficult

5			1				6	
			7			4		1
2				8			3	
		9			3		5	
		7				9		
	6		2			3		
	4			9				5
9		1			5			
	5				7			8

Su Doku

	3				5		8	9
8	1				4			7
	6					5		
5			9	7				
				3	8			1
		9					7	
6			1				4	8
4	5		3				9	

Difficult

		6			1			5
			9				1	
3				7			8	
2		7			3			
		5	8		9	6		
			2			5		8
	9			8				1
	4				5			
5			1			2		

			7	8				
6							7	
9						1		4
4	3			6			8	
		7		2		9		
	8			4			1	3
7		6						8
	5							2
				5	3			

Difficult

	5			3			9	
		2		8		5		
3		9				6		2
	2						1	
7			4		3			9
	3						7	
6		3				9		8
		4		9		2		
	9			5			3	

Su Doku

9			4			1		8
	4						7	
6				8	7			
		3	9		5			2
		1				6		
7			2		6	4		
			8	5				1
	3						4	
1		6			4			7

Difficult

2		5	8					6
6							8	7
	7		6		2	4		
		2	4		3	5		
		9	1		7		6	
7	9							8
3					1	6		5

Su Doku

		2	7					
			3	8	9		2	7
							8	4
						6		
	6	9	2		1	8	3	
		8						
1	8							
6	7		4	1	3			
					6	7		

Difficult

	2		1	6		5	9	
		8						
						8	1	6
			3				4	1
		4	9		6	7		
1	3				2			
3	9	5						
						6		
	6	1		9	7		2	

				3	2	8		
		4	1					
3		8			7	4	5	
6		2					4	
1								7
	7					5		8
	3	6	7			1		9
					1	3		
		1	9	8				

Difficult

6	3		4				1	
			6		8	4		
4				9	1			
						1	6	
7								8
	4	2						
			8	7				2
		8	3		2			
	7				5		8	4

Su Doku

	7		2	1				6
					6		3	
9		3			7		2	
5	1							
2				6				1
							4	3
	8		1			7		2
	5		6					
1				2	8		9	

Difficult

8								
		4	8			1	7	
	9	7			1			
2			4		9		3	
		6				2		
	1		6		8			9
			7			4	9	
	8	5			2	6		
								3

Su Doku

5			4		9		3	
	8	4		7			2	
		2						
3			2			1		
		8		5		2		
		6			8			3
						4		
	6			4		8	5	
	2		9		7			6

Difficult

	6			5			8	
	5		4		8		7	
	2		7		6		9	
		5		7		9		
		7				5		
		1		6		8		
	8		5		7		6	
	1		9		2		3	
	7			3			5	

4	5			7		3		
			5		8	2		
1								
	1		9				2	
9								4
	3				1		9	
								5
		1	4		7			
		6		1			4	3

Difficult

3	8						9	2
	4	6				5	8	
			6		5			
5				6				8
		1				3		
8				2				7
			2		9			
	5	8				9	7	
1	3						2	5

		2			6	7	8	
			9		8			6
	8		7			3		
	5							8
7			3		4			1
4							2	
		5			7		6	
2			8		5			
	1	9	4			5		

Difficult

					7		2	
2		6		4				
			2		3	7		
3			6				5	
9		7				1		6
	2				9			4
		3	1		5			
				3		4		5
	8		7					

Su Doku

		1			6		7	
9								
		6	5		9	4		3
3		8		1		7		
			9		8			
		7		2		8		4
5		3	8		2	6		
								7
	4		7			9		

Difficult

	5		9				7	
	4	8						
7			5		6	4		
1	6	7	8	3				
				1	2	3	4	6
		6	2		9			8
						2	9	
	8				3		5	

Su Doku

				5	6			
	5			8			9	
		8	9		4	2		
9		1				3		
7	8						5	6
		5				1		7
		3	1		7	4		
	2			9			3	
			5	3				

Difficult

	8			2			4	
2		3				6		5
4		9				3		7
			4		2			
		8	6		3	5		
			9		5			
5		6				4		8
8		4				7		9
	3			9			5	

Su Doku

	1	5		4		6	3	
			8		3			
	9						2	
6		9				2		4
	8						9	
5		3				7		1
	3						4	
			9		6			
	6	8		1		3	7	

		4						
2		3	8		7			
	6		9			3		
			3		9	7		4
	2						9	
4		6	2		5			
		8			6		1	
			4		3	8		5
						4		

Su Doku

9	2		7	8				
		1			9			
	8						1	
8					5			2
1		4				5		8
5			6					4
	7						9	
			3			6		
				4	7		8	3

Difficult

5		6						4
	3				8			
	8		6	4	7		1	
		3					9	7
				9				
6	5					1		
	7		9	8	3		6	
			1				8	
1						7		3

Su Doku

2								1
8	1						6	2
	7		6		2		5	
		1		6		2		
			3		1			
		3		4		1		
	8		7		9		2	
9	3						4	8
5								9

Difficult

		2						3
6		7			9		2	
	9	1		5				
	7		1	9				
8								9
				2	7		5	
				6		2	3	
	4		2			9		7
2						4		

Su Doku

3		4		7		8		9
		8				6		
	9						4	
2		6	1		8	9		5
4		5	2		3	1		6
	4						6	
		9				2		
1		2		6		7		3

		1					5	2
4			3			1		
				7	1			9
	6		5					
		8	7	1	9	2		
					2		7	
9			8	3				
		6			5			3
5	2					6		

Su Doku

		4		7		5		
			1			6	9	
			3		9		8	
	8					7		3
	3			9			1	
2		1					6	
	4		9		3			
	6	9			5			
		2		6		1		

Difficult

					3	4		
		9	2	4				
6						2		
2			1				9	3
		1	4		8	6		
7	6				5			2
		7						6
				5	1	3		
		2	6					

Su Doku

8		3				9		1
	5		4		9		2	
3			9		1			2
	1		8		5		7	
5			2		4			3
	7		5		2		3	
4		2				8		6

Difficult

			9		2	5	4	
		3		6				7
2								
6			3			7		
1				9				6
		2			6			5
								1
4				7		9		
	7	6	2		4			

8	1						5	
5		2		6	9			
				2			1	3
	7		9					
		4				5		
					6		8	
9	8			7				
			3	8		2		5
	4						7	8

Difficult

1			8				6	
					5		3	9
			3				2	
						3		6
8		6	5		1	2		4
4		2						
	8			6				
2	7		4					
	5				9			8

Su Doku

7	8				4	9		
	4			3				
9				2			1	3
			5			1	8	
				6				
	1	6			7			
4	5			7				9
				8			4	
		8	4				3	2

Difficult

		2		1	7		8	3
						2		
9				2				7
	2						6	5
			2		6			
1	3						2	
7				8				6
		9						
8	6		5	7		3		

Su Doku

		3	6		4	1		
		6	7		1	2		
	7			8			3	
9		7				3		8
2		1				9		5
	6			9			1	
		5	3		6	8		
		9	2		5	6		

Difficult

5							9	
		3		7				
	1				5	6		
				3	7		5	
8			6		9			7
	9		1	2				
		2	3				8	
				4		9		
	6							3

Su Doku

	6						2	
5		9		3		8		7
			6	7	9			
3			8		1			9
	1						5	
2			7		6			8
			4	2	7			
9		7		6		4		1
	5						7	

Difficult

5	8						4	9
			8		1			
	7			6			1	
8								1
	2	4	5		6	3	9	
7								6
	1			2			6	
			9		3			
3	4						8	7

8	7							2
							7	
6			9	4			3	1
3		1	7					
				2				
					3	1		9
9	4			5	8			7
	2							
1							5	6

Difficult

				8				
			3				5	6
		8		5			7	3
	6		7		1		2	
	4						3	
	8		6		9		4	
5	1			6		2		
9	7				5			
				9				

Su Doku

			1		9			6
				7	3		4	
	3					5		
8		1		2				9
	4						5	
2				1		4		3
		5					6	
	7		9	5				
1			7		8			

Difficult

				2		1	4	
					5			
4	7	5						
	5				6	8	2	
3			8		2			9
	8	9	4				3	
						5	8	7
			5					
	6	3		9				

Su Doku

				5	8			
7					1			4
		3	6			7		
9							3	
6	1		9		7		8	5
	3							2
		1			6	3		
4			1					8
			5	2				

Difficult

4	5			1			7	
		1	6	9			2	
	4	7			1			3
	1		9		5		4	
5			2			8	9	
	6			4	9	1		
	9			8			6	5

Su Doku

						6		
6					4	1		8
3	4		8				7	
					2	7	3	
	7			5			9	
	3	8	9					
	8				9		2	6
5		6	3					7
		2						

	5						3	
			8	3	1			
	1		2		9		6	
9			4		2			3
		4				5		
8			1		5			6
	3		5		8		2	
			6	1	4			
	4						5	

Su Doku

		3						
			1		7			
7		4	6				8	3
	2					1		8
4	5		2		1		7	6
1		7					2	
3	4				9	6		1
			3		5			
						7		

Difficult

			5		7			
4		6				5		7
	5		9	6	2		1	
9								4
		2		7		1		
6								5
	3		4	9	8		5	
1		5				7		9
			7		5			

Su Doku

		2	8		5	1		
	5		9		7		3	
		3		6		5		
	3			9			5	
8								6
	1			8			7	
		8		7		6		
	2		6		3		8	
		1	5		8	2		

Difficult

7	6	4		9				
		1	4					5
8		3			6			
			9	4			8	
6								7
	4			2	7			
			8			6		2
2					4	8		
			7			1	5	4

	6	4		1	5			
			3					7
		9			6	4		3
		5			3		6	
	9						8	
	4		8			7		
8		1	6			9		
9					7			
			9	5		1	3	

Difficult

	5			2			7	
		1				8		
	6		1		9		5	
		9	3		5	6		
6				8				3
		5	9		2	7		
	7		8		1		3	
		3				9		
	9			7			6	

Su Doku

			9			3		7
	4		8		2	6		
	3		4					
	8		6			2		
		3				9		
		6			9		8	
					6		1	
		7	2		1		9	
5		2			4			

		8				7		
	3			5			1	
5			1		6			2
1				2				4
	6		7		4		2	
4				8				3
2			5		3			7
	7			1			9	
		6				2		

	9			3			5	
1								8
	7		5		8		2	
		1	6		4	7		
	4						3	
		7	3		2	4		
	3		8		5		9	
5								6
	8			9			7	

Difficult

			5	1	7			
	8						2	
4		7				1		6
	5		8		9		6	
9								3
	7		4		3		8	
3		5				6		4
	9						1	
			2	9	6			

Su Doku

				9	4			
	9					2		5
	5					8		3
8			3			7		
			1	6	9			
		3			8			9
3		4					8	
9		6					7	
			2	7				

	1		2				7	
		8			4			
				5			9	2
			9			1	5	4
7	9	5			6			
2	8			9				
			3			9		
	6				7		3	

Su Doku

	1				2	8	3	
9		7					5	
				4	1			
6	3					2		
		2		8		5		
		8					1	9
			6	5				
	5					1		8
	7	4	8				6	

5		8	7					2
				3			6	
					5		3	7
					7		4	
9		4				6		1
	1		8					
8	9		2					
	7			4				
4					8	9		3

Su Doku

		2		3				
				6	4			
4	5					2		
1				2	3	8		
6			4		8			3
		8	7	1				2
		3					7	6
			1	4				
				9		4		

Difficult

			7	8			6	
				6		2	7	
	8		1			4		
		1				9		
6				3				1
		2				6		
		8			1		5	
	7	5		9				
	9			5	3			

Su Doku

		3		2				4
		4			7			2
7	6				3			
	9				8	1		
2								7
		7	1				8	
			7				1	6
1			5			7		
6				9		5		

Difficult

	2		7	3	4			
8		4			9	7		
				6				
		2		9		6	3	
		1				5		
	5	6		8		2		
				7				
		7	9			8		6
			6	2	1		9	

Su Doku

						1		
			7	5	9			
7		8		4		3		
	8		4		2		6	
	2	7		9		8	4	
	4		3		8		1	
		5		2		6		1
			8	1	4			
		1						

		1	8	9	5	7		
	4		7		1		3	
	7	5				4	2	
		6		7		5		
	2	8				9	7	
	1		6		2		9	
		7	1	4	3	8		

Su Doku

			2		8			
1								8
	8	2	5		6	9	4	
3		4				6		7
	7						1	
8		5				2		4
	3	7	9		4	1	6	
5								9
			7		1			

Difficult

6			9		1			8
		5			4	9		
	8				3		5	
7	5	6						9
3						8	6	2
	7		3				2	
		1	5			3		
9			6		7			1

1							7	
				2				
		5	8		1	3		2
		8		3			9	
3			4		7			8
	9			5		2		
2		6	3		5	8		
				4				
	5							7

Difficult

							1	3
			5				8	
	7	2	6		1	5		
				1			4	2
1								6
6	2			3				
		8	1		2	7	5	
	9				5			
5	1							

Su Doku

1					4		8	
		7						6
	4		6		8	1		3
				9			5	
6				1				4
	3			4				
8		2	7		3		4	
3						8		
	7		2					9

Difficult

	5			9			6	
6	8						4	2
		2				8		
4			1		2			6
	6						5	
5			7		6			8
		6				5		
7	4						3	9
	2			3			1	

Su Doku

	3						2	
		7	3		8	1		
2								5
	7		6		2		8	
		2	9		1	7		
	9		7		3		6	
4								7
		9	1		4	2		
	8						3	

Difficult

		7		3			8	
			9				2	
1	4		7					
6				4	9	1		
				5				
		8	3	6				4
					8		9	2
	6				4			
	8			9		5		

	3	2	6		5	1		9
		8						
7	6		3					
				1		9		
9	5						7	3
		6		5				
					4		1	8
						4		
8		4	1		9	3	5	

Difficult

9			8			4		
7			9					6
	1			2		7		
1			5					
	7	4				8	1	
					2			5
		3		7			2	
4					8			7
		7			3			9

Su Doku

6					2	1	9	
	3						5	
		1			8			7
5				9				
			6	5	7			
				3				6
7			1			4		
	9						1	
	2	6	9					5

Difficult

	3			2			1	
5	1	8				7	6	2
		4	8		2	5		
			9		7			
		7	6		1	4		
7	4	1				9	3	8
	9			7			2	

Su Doku

3				6				7
		8		4	2	3		
	2				7		8	
	5	3						
8	6						5	3
						7	1	
	4		9				3	
		5	6	7		1		
2				5				8

Difficult

	7						6	
		1		5		4		
		8	3		7	9		
	3		4		8		9	
	8			6				4
	4		1		9			5
		2	9		3	5		
		4		7		6		
	9						8	

Su Doku

		8		9		5		
	1			8			2	
3			6		2			9
		3				4		
	5		8		7		6	
		2				9		
2			3		4			8
	7			2			4	
		6		1		2		

Difficult

4		9				6	2	
			5	3				
6	8							
	2			1	3	8		
			6		4			
		7	8	5			9	
							4	6
				4	7			
	4	8				7		3

Su Doku

9								8
	4	1				2	7	
			3		5			
		9		4		8		
2	8		7		9		1	6
		4		3		5		
			2		6			
	2	7				9	6	
1								5

Difficult

				5				
	1	2				3	4	
9								6
2			5		9			8
	5	1		6		4	7	
4			7		3			5
1								2
	8	4				9	6	
				7				

Su Doku

			6				3	7
4			2	9				6
			1		2			4
				6	1			5
		1				7		
2			9	8				
5		7		3				
1				7	9			8
6	4				8			

Difficult

		4	9				7	5
8			2					
7					6	8	3	
5		2						
6				8				9
						6		2
	8	3	1					7
					4			1
2	5				9	4		

Su Doku

						7		
		6	3		9	1		
1	8		6				9	
	6		9		4	8	2	
	3	9	5		1		6	
	9				7		4	1
		4	1		2	5		
		2						

Difficult

4			7	6	3			1
3		7				4		6
	1		3	5	9		8	
5								9
	8		6	4	2		1	
8		1				6		2
6			5	7	8			3

Su Doku

	9			1			3	
4			8			6		1
	1	7	9			2		
						5	2	
1				9				3
	7	5						
		1			9	4	8	
7		6			4			2
	2			8			5	

Difficult

9	5		8					
	4					7		8
			1	2				4
6	8			4				
			2		8			
			3				1	5
2				1	9			
8		7					9	
				3			6	2

Su Doku

		2						
		1			6			
3	9		5	4				7
6		7		3			5	
		3				9		
	2			8		6		3
8				5	1		9	6
			9			2		
						3		

Difficult

				5			3	
4			9		1	8		
	9				3			
	8	2	1		9		4	
6								7
	4		7		2	1	6	
			4				5	
		4	3		7			6
	1			8				

Su Doku

6	2	5		7	1			
			8					5
	1			2				6
		7						4
		6				9		
2						8		
3				5			6	
7					6			
			4	9		2	1	3

Difficult

		3				9		
	9		3		5		6	
		6		8		3		
	3		7		1		9	
		5		6		1		
	2		5		3			7
		4		3		2		
	8		1		6		5	
		2				6		

Su Doku

3	8						9	2
		2				8		
		4	2		9	1		
	9		7		3		6	
		3				2		
	4		8		5		3	
		8	5		6	3		
		9				6		
6	7						2	4

Difficult

					6		5	
		3	8			9		7
8							4	
				6	9	3		5
2		6				7		8
3		9	7	2				
	1							6
5		7			1	2		
	2		3					

Su Doku

	5				7	1		
			8		1			5
1		8				7		
3	9			4			7	
			3		9			
	6			8			3	9
		6				5		3
5			7		8			
		2	9				6	

Difficult

		1						
	8					6	1	
	6		7	8	1			4
		4	3		7	8		
		9				1		
		8	5		2	3		
4			6	3	9		7	
	5	7					9	
						2		

Su Doku

	6				2		5	
				7	3			
3		7			4		9	
8				2			7	
7								1
	4			6				5
	9		3			1		8
			2	1				
	2		5				6	

Difficult

1								2
			4	9	3			
	5	8				4	3	
	3		6		7		1	
5								9
	8		3		9		2	
	2	7				5	6	
			7	6	8			
6								1

Su Doku

5		9		2		1		8
8			9		6			7
	7	5				4	3	
			2		3			
	9	1				2	8	
7			6		5			4
9		2		7		8		3

Difficult

1	8		3					9
		7		4	8			5
			7				4	
	2							4
	9	5				6	3	
6							8	
	7			8				
2			5	6		4		
4					3		1	8

Su Doku

		3	2	7	1	8		
	2		4		9		7	
2	9			5			8	6
		5				7		
1	6			8			4	9
	7		6		3		5	
		1	8	9	5	4		

Difficult

	7					1	4	
1		2						7
9					8		5	
		4	5	2	6			
			3		4			
			9	8	7	5		
	6		7					1
2						4		8
	3	9					6	

Su Doku

3	1		7					
	5		3	1				
6		9				3		
		7			9			
8				2				6
			1			5		
		8				2		5
				3	2		4	
					1		7	3

Difficult

9					3	1	5		6
5	6					9			
									4
		5				2	1		
	9							4	
		1	3				2		
2									
			6					8	7
8		3	4	9					1

Su Doku

1		5	8			9		
					9		7	
			1	5				6
8	6		5					
3								4
					2		5	1
2				9	6			
	8		3					
		4			8	6		2

Difficult

					3			
5	2				6			1
4	7	3			5	8		
7			3					4
		5				7		
2					1			9
		2	8			4	9	6
3			5				1	7
			9					

Su Doku

					9		3	
3	1			2		4		
					1		5	
5			1		7	3		
	3						9	
		8	4		2			5
	5		6					
		3		5			2	4
	7		2					

Difficult

	3							
			3			8	7	6
			8	5	9		2	
8	4					5		2
2								3
6		5					8	4
	1		9	2	8			
3	8	7			1			
							1	

Su Doku

		6	9	8				1
9	3		4					
					6			8
		4			5		8	
8								3
	2		7			9		
3			6					
					2		5	4
4				9	1	6		

Difficult

							3	2
		8	9		3			1
					4	5		
7			6	9				
6		9				4		8
				5	7			9
		1	7					
4			1		2	9		
9	2							

Su Doku

		4	7					
		2	8		6			
		3				6	9	7
	6		4		3		5	2
4	3		9		5		8	
8	4	6				1		
			2		1	5		
					4	8		

Difficult

					3	6	5	
1		2					3	
	3		7		2			
			1			9	4	
		1				3		
	4	5			8			
			8		7		6	
	1					5		7
	9	6	4					

Su Doku

	4			8			9	
5		1				8		3
	8			3			2	
9			1		8			4
2			3		4			9
	2			7			5	
1		8				9		6
	7			1			3	

Difficult

			4			2		
	2		8			3	1	
7	6			1				
			7		8		5	3
		6				9		
3	9		6		5			
				8			9	1
	7	5			6		3	
		1			9			

Su Doku

7		8	4					
			9	3				
	1	6			7			
5						3	2	7
4								8
1	7	2						5
			7			2	5	
				6	8			
					4	7		9

Difficult

1			8		6			
7			5	1				
8	3		9			5		
		5					3	
	2						1	
	6					2		
		8			9		2	7
				3	1			4
			7		8			6

Su Doku

8		3				7		1
			3		7			
	2						5	
	8	9		1		5	4	
	1						9	
	3	2		4		1	8	
	6						1	
			1		9			
5		1				6		4

Difficult

			2					1
			9			7	6	
4	7	1						
			5				1	8
	4	8				5	2	
5	3				4			
						9	3	2
	6	4			2			
7					8			

Su Doku

				4			6	
		6			8	5		
8					6	7		
2			9				3	7
	7						2	
6	4				5			8
		1	6					4
		7	8			1		
	5			1				

Difficult

	1		2	3	6		4	
	3		1	8	7		5	
		9		6		4		
5		2				1		9
		7		9		8		
	5		6	7	3		9	
	7		9	1	4		3	

Su Doku

Solutions

1

4	9	6	1	5	7	8	2	3
2	7	8	4	3	9	5	1	6
3	1	5	2	8	6	9	7	4
9	4	2	3	6	8	1	5	7
6	3	7	9	1	5	4	8	2
8	5	1	7	2	4	6	3	9
5	8	4	6	7	2	3	9	1
1	2	9	5	4	3	7	6	8
7	6	3	8	9	1	2	4	5

2

9	2	7	8	1	6	4	5	3
5	4	6	7	9	3	8	2	1
3	8	1	4	5	2	9	6	7
4	7	2	5	6	9	3	1	8
6	9	5	1	3	8	2	7	4
1	3	8	2	4	7	6	9	5
8	6	3	9	7	1	5	4	2
7	5	9	3	2	4	1	8	6
2	1	4	6	8	5	7	3	9

Solutions

3

4	3	5	1	9	6	2	8	7
8	1	9	7	5	2	3	6	4
7	6	2	8	3	4	1	9	5
9	2	1	6	4	8	5	7	3
6	4	7	5	2	3	8	1	9
3	5	8	9	7	1	6	4	2
2	9	6	3	8	7	4	5	1
1	7	3	4	6	5	9	2	8
5	8	4	2	1	9	7	3	6

4

6	3	9	1	5	4	8	2	7
8	2	1	7	6	3	5	9	4
4	7	5	9	8	2	1	3	6
1	8	7	3	9	6	4	5	2
5	4	3	2	7	1	9	6	8
2	9	6	5	4	8	3	7	1
3	6	8	4	2	5	7	1	9
9	5	4	6	1	7	2	8	3
7	1	2	8	3	9	6	4	5

Solutions

5

9	7	2	3	5	6	4	1	8
4	5	3	2	8	1	9	7	6
6	8	1	9	4	7	2	5	3
3	2	6	8	9	5	1	4	7
1	4	7	6	2	3	8	9	5
8	9	5	7	1	4	3	6	2
5	6	9	4	3	8	7	2	1
2	1	8	5	7	9	6	3	4
7	3	4	1	6	2	5	8	9

6

3	5	1	9	6	7	4	8	2
6	9	8	1	4	2	5	7	3
4	2	7	3	5	8	1	9	6
9	3	6	4	1	5	8	2	7
2	1	5	8	7	3	9	6	4
7	8	4	2	9	6	3	5	1
5	4	2	7	3	9	6	1	8
8	6	3	5	2	1	7	4	9
1	7	9	6	8	4	2	3	5

Solutions

7

3	4	5	1	2	8	6	7	9
1	7	9	4	3	6	5	2	8
2	6	8	5	9	7	1	4	3
4	9	1	7	6	2	3	8	5
8	2	7	9	5	3	4	6	1
5	3	6	8	1	4	7	9	2
6	5	4	3	8	9	2	1	7
7	8	3	2	4	1	9	5	6
9	1	2	6	7	5	8	3	4

8

7	1	2	6	4	9	8	5	3
5	8	3	7	1	2	9	6	4
9	4	6	8	3	5	7	1	2
2	5	9	1	7	4	6	3	8
1	6	7	9	8	3	2	4	5
8	3	4	5	2	6	1	7	9
3	9	5	2	6	1	4	8	7
6	2	8	4	5	7	3	9	1
4	7	1	3	9	8	5	2	6

Solutions

9

2	5	3	9	7	4	1	6	8
4	8	7	3	6	1	9	5	2
1	6	9	2	8	5	4	3	7
6	9	2	1	3	8	5	7	4
5	1	4	6	9	7	8	2	3
7	3	8	4	5	2	6	1	9
9	7	6	5	4	3	2	8	1
3	4	1	8	2	6	7	9	5
8	2	5	7	1	9	3	4	6

10

2	6	5	3	1	9	4	7	8
8	9	7	2	5	4	6	3	1
3	4	1	7	8	6	9	5	2
9	7	2	6	4	5	1	8	3
1	8	4	9	2	3	7	6	5
6	5	3	8	7	1	2	4	9
7	1	9	4	3	8	5	2	6
4	3	6	5	9	2	8	1	7
5	2	8	1	6	7	3	9	4

Solutions

11

9	1	4	7	2	6	3	8	5
5	6	8	1	3	9	2	7	4
3	7	2	8	4	5	9	1	6
1	4	6	3	9	2	8	5	7
8	2	3	4	5	7	1	6	9
7	5	9	6	8	1	4	2	3
6	3	5	9	1	8	7	4	2
4	8	7	2	6	3	5	9	1
2	9	1	5	7	4	6	3	8

12

7	4	8	3	1	2	9	6	5
3	2	1	5	9	6	4	7	8
9	5	6	4	7	8	3	2	1
8	1	4	7	2	5	6	3	9
5	9	7	1	6	3	8	4	2
2	6	3	9	8	4	5	1	7
6	3	9	2	5	7	1	8	4
1	8	2	6	4	9	7	5	3
4	7	5	8	3	1	2	9	6

Solutions

13

4	8	9	7	2	1	5	3	6
5	3	7	9	8	6	2	4	1
1	6	2	5	4	3	8	9	7
9	2	3	8	7	4	6	1	5
6	1	4	2	3	5	7	8	9
7	5	8	1	6	9	4	2	3
2	4	5	3	9	7	1	6	8
8	9	1	6	5	2	3	7	4
3	7	6	4	1	8	9	5	2

14

4	1	7	5	8	3	6	2	9
6	8	5	1	9	2	7	4	3
2	3	9	7	6	4	1	8	5
8	7	6	3	4	1	5	9	2
3	5	2	9	7	8	4	6	1
9	4	1	2	5	6	3	7	8
7	6	3	8	1	9	2	5	4
1	9	4	6	2	5	8	3	7
5	2	8	4	3	7	9	1	6

Solutions

15

9	5	4	7	8	2	6	1	3
7	8	1	9	3	6	2	4	5
2	3	6	1	4	5	8	7	9
1	4	9	6	2	8	3	5	7
3	6	2	4	5	7	9	8	1
5	7	8	3	1	9	4	2	6
8	2	3	5	9	1	7	6	4
6	9	5	8	7	4	1	3	2
4	1	7	2	6	3	5	9	8

16

8	4	3	2	1	5	7	6	9
2	5	1	7	9	6	8	3	4
6	9	7	3	8	4	5	2	1
3	8	6	9	2	7	4	1	5
5	1	2	4	3	8	9	7	6
9	7	4	6	5	1	3	8	2
4	3	9	8	6	2	1	5	7
7	6	5	1	4	3	2	9	8
1	2	8	5	7	9	6	4	3

Solutions

3	8	5	1	4	9	7	2	6
2	7	4	3	5	6	9	1	8
9	1	6	2	8	7	4	3	5
6	9	1	4	2	5	8	7	3
5	4	7	6	3	8	2	9	1
8	2	3	9	7	1	6	5	4
4	5	2	8	9	3	1	6	7
7	6	8	5	1	2	3	4	9
1	3	9	7	6	4	5	8	2

9	6	8	3	1	7	5	4	2
1	3	4	8	2	5	6	9	7
7	5	2	6	4	9	1	3	8
2	1	5	7	9	8	3	6	4
3	9	7	5	6	4	8	2	1
8	4	6	2	3	1	9	7	5
5	8	9	4	7	6	2	1	3
6	7	3	1	5	2	4	8	9
4	2	1	9	8	3	7	5	6

Solutions

19

1	2	7	4	3	8	5	6	9
4	3	9	1	5	6	8	2	7
5	6	8	7	9	2	3	4	1
3	4	1	9	6	5	2	7	8
6	9	5	2	8	7	4	1	3
7	8	2	3	4	1	9	5	6
2	7	3	8	1	4	6	9	5
9	1	6	5	2	3	7	8	4
8	5	4	6	7	9	1	3	2

20

3	8	5	4	6	7	9	2	1
7	1	2	5	3	9	8	6	4
4	6	9	8	1	2	7	5	3
5	9	4	2	7	3	1	8	6
8	7	1	9	4	6	2	3	5
2	3	6	1	5	8	4	7	9
6	5	8	7	9	4	3	1	2
1	4	7	3	2	5	6	9	8
9	2	3	6	8	1	5	4	7

Solutions

21

5	6	7	2	3	4	1	8	9
2	9	1	6	5	8	7	4	3
8	4	3	7	1	9	2	6	5
9	1	6	3	8	2	4	5	7
7	2	4	1	6	5	9	3	8
3	5	8	9	4	7	6	2	1
4	8	9	5	7	6	3	1	2
1	7	5	4	2	3	8	9	6
6	3	2	8	9	1	5	7	4

22

1	7	9	5	4	6	3	8	2
8	6	3	1	9	2	4	5	7
5	2	4	8	3	7	1	9	6
6	8	1	2	7	4	5	3	9
7	4	2	9	5	3	6	1	8
3	9	5	6	1	8	7	2	4
9	1	7	4	2	5	8	6	3
2	3	8	7	6	1	9	4	5
4	5	6	3	8	9	2	7	1

23

2	6	4	3	8	7	1	9	5
3	8	9	5	6	1	7	4	2
1	7	5	4	9	2	6	3	8
6	4	2	8	5	9	3	7	1
7	1	3	2	4	6	5	8	9
9	5	8	1	7	3	4	2	6
4	9	6	7	1	8	2	5	3
5	3	1	9	2	4	8	6	7
8	2	7	6	3	5	9	1	4

24

4	8	7	9	1	2	3	6	5
3	6	5	7	8	4	1	9	2
9	1	2	6	3	5	4	8	7
5	2	6	1	7	8	9	3	4
1	9	4	2	6	3	7	5	8
8	7	3	4	5	9	2	1	6
6	5	9	3	2	7	8	4	1
7	4	1	8	9	6	5	2	3
2	3	8	5	4	1	6	7	9

Solutions

25

8	3	1	6	2	5	9	4	7
2	6	4	9	7	8	5	3	1
5	7	9	1	4	3	2	6	8
9	2	7	5	1	4	6	8	3
3	8	5	2	6	7	1	9	4
1	4	6	8	3	9	7	2	5
7	9	3	4	5	6	8	1	2
4	1	8	7	9	2	3	5	6
6	5	2	3	8	1	4	7	9

26

9	1	3	2	6	5	4	8	7
4	7	2	8	9	1	3	6	5
8	5	6	3	7	4	9	2	1
2	8	1	7	3	9	6	5	4
3	6	4	1	5	2	7	9	8
7	9	5	6	4	8	2	1	3
5	2	9	4	1	3	8	7	6
1	3	7	9	8	6	5	4	2
6	4	8	5	2	7	1	3	9

27

5	4	1	2	6	9	7	3	8
7	3	6	1	8	4	9	5	2
2	8	9	7	5	3	6	1	4
4	1	7	9	3	8	5	2	6
9	5	8	4	2	6	1	7	3
3	6	2	5	1	7	4	8	9
6	7	3	8	4	1	2	9	5
8	9	5	6	7	2	3	4	1
1	2	4	3	9	5	8	6	7

28

9	5	3	1	4	2	8	7	6
8	6	2	3	5	7	1	9	4
4	7	1	8	9	6	3	5	2
7	2	9	6	3	1	5	4	8
6	4	5	2	8	9	7	1	3
1	3	8	5	7	4	6	2	9
2	1	4	7	6	8	9	3	5
5	9	6	4	1	3	2	8	7
3	8	7	9	2	5	4	6	1

Solutions

29

2	3	7	8	9	5	1	6	4
4	6	9	1	2	3	7	5	8
1	8	5	4	7	6	9	3	2
6	7	8	5	4	1	2	9	3
3	5	2	7	8	9	4	1	6
9	4	1	6	3	2	5	8	7
5	2	4	3	1	8	6	7	9
7	1	3	9	6	4	8	2	5
8	9	6	2	5	7	3	4	1

30

2	1	8	9	4	7	6	3	5
7	9	4	3	6	5	1	8	2
6	5	3	8	1	2	7	9	4
4	8	9	7	3	1	2	5	6
5	3	6	4	2	8	9	1	7
1	7	2	5	9	6	3	4	8
9	2	5	1	7	4	8	6	3
3	4	7	6	8	9	5	2	1
8	6	1	2	5	3	4	7	9

Solutions

31

3	7	6	2	1	9	8	4	5
1	4	5	6	3	8	7	9	2
8	2	9	5	7	4	6	3	1
7	9	1	8	2	5	3	6	4
4	5	2	7	6	3	1	8	9
6	3	8	9	4	1	2	5	7
2	6	4	3	5	7	9	1	8
5	8	7	1	9	6	4	2	3
9	1	3	4	8	2	5	7	6

32

1	6	2	9	3	8	5	4	7
8	3	9	5	7	4	6	1	2
5	4	7	1	2	6	8	3	9
6	7	4	2	8	1	3	9	5
3	2	8	7	5	9	4	6	1
9	1	5	6	4	3	2	7	8
2	5	6	3	1	7	9	8	4
4	9	1	8	6	5	7	2	3
7	8	3	4	9	2	1	5	6

Solutions

33

1	8	9	3	6	5	7	2	4
6	2	7	1	4	9	8	3	5
4	3	5	2	7	8	6	1	9
2	6	8	5	9	7	3	4	1
5	9	4	6	3	1	2	7	8
7	1	3	4	8	2	9	5	6
3	7	1	8	5	6	4	9	2
9	5	6	7	2	4	1	8	3
8	4	2	9	1	3	5	6	7

34

8	7	1	9	4	3	2	5	6
2	5	9	8	1	6	7	3	4
4	6	3	7	2	5	1	8	9
9	3	2	1	6	4	5	7	8
5	4	7	2	3	8	6	9	1
6	1	8	5	9	7	4	2	3
7	9	5	4	8	1	3	6	2
3	8	4	6	5	2	9	1	7
1	2	6	3	7	9	8	4	5

35

5	8	6	4	2	9	1	3	7
9	7	2	6	1	3	4	8	5
1	3	4	7	8	5	9	6	2
2	6	9	1	5	8	7	4	3
7	4	8	9	3	6	2	5	1
3	5	1	2	7	4	8	9	6
8	9	7	3	6	1	5	2	4
4	1	3	5	9	2	6	7	8
6	2	5	8	4	7	3	1	9

36

4	1	7	8	9	6	5	3	2
2	6	3	4	1	5	8	7	9
5	8	9	7	2	3	6	4	1
8	9	6	5	4	7	2	1	3
7	5	1	2	3	8	9	6	4
3	4	2	9	6	1	7	8	5
9	2	8	3	7	4	1	5	6
6	3	5	1	8	2	4	9	7
1	7	4	6	5	9	3	2	8

Solutions

37

5	3	9	8	1	4	6	7	2
1	4	2	9	6	7	3	8	5
8	7	6	2	3	5	1	4	9
9	5	7	1	4	6	8	2	3
2	8	1	3	5	9	7	6	4
3	6	4	7	2	8	5	9	1
7	1	8	4	9	3	2	5	6
4	2	5	6	8	1	9	3	7
6	9	3	5	7	2	4	1	8

38

9	8	4	2	1	7	5	3	6
3	5	7	6	8	4	1	2	9
1	6	2	5	3	9	4	7	8
6	7	1	4	9	3	8	5	2
4	9	5	1	2	8	7	6	3
8	2	3	7	5	6	9	1	4
5	1	8	3	4	2	6	9	7
7	3	9	8	6	1	2	4	5
2	4	6	9	7	5	3	8	1

Solutions

9	6	8	5	3	7	1	4	2
5	7	4	2	9	1	8	3	6
2	1	3	4	8	6	9	7	5
8	4	5	1	6	2	7	9	3
6	2	7	9	4	3	5	1	8
3	9	1	7	5	8	6	2	4
4	8	6	3	7	9	2	5	1
7	3	2	8	1	5	4	6	9
1	5	9	6	2	4	3	8	7

5	3	7	8	2	1	9	4	6
4	1	8	3	6	9	2	5	7
9	2	6	7	5	4	1	3	8
2	6	3	9	7	5	4	8	1
1	9	4	2	8	3	7	6	5
7	8	5	4	1	6	3	9	2
6	7	9	1	3	8	5	2	4
8	4	1	5	9	2	6	7	3
3	5	2	6	4	7	8	1	9

Solutions

41

3	7	6	2	1	9	4	8	5
5	8	2	4	6	3	7	1	9
1	4	9	8	5	7	2	6	3
4	2	7	3	9	1	8	5	6
9	1	8	6	4	5	3	7	2
6	5	3	7	2	8	1	9	4
8	9	5	1	3	2	6	4	7
2	6	1	5	7	4	9	3	8
7	3	4	9	8	6	5	2	1

42

3	1	4	9	5	6	8	7	2
7	6	2	1	4	8	9	5	3
8	9	5	3	7	2	4	6	1
5	7	8	2	1	3	6	4	9
1	3	6	5	9	4	7	2	8
2	4	9	6	8	7	3	1	5
9	5	7	4	3	1	2	8	6
4	2	1	8	6	9	5	3	7
6	8	3	7	2	5	1	9	4

43

3	8	9	4	2	1	6	7	5
6	4	1	3	5	7	8	9	2
2	5	7	6	9	8	1	4	3
7	2	6	8	1	3	9	5	4
9	3	5	2	4	6	7	8	1
4	1	8	9	7	5	3	2	6
8	9	4	1	3	2	5	6	7
1	7	2	5	6	9	4	3	8
5	6	3	7	8	4	2	1	9

44

2	4	9	1	5	3	7	8	6
1	3	5	7	8	6	4	9	2
6	7	8	2	9	4	3	1	5
8	6	7	5	4	2	1	3	9
9	2	3	6	1	8	5	7	4
4	5	1	3	7	9	6	2	8
5	9	6	8	3	1	2	4	7
3	8	2	4	6	7	9	5	1
7	1	4	9	2	5	8	6	3

Solutions

45

4	3	9	6	2	8	5	1	7
2	7	5	9	3	1	6	8	4
8	6	1	5	4	7	3	2	9
6	9	8	4	7	3	2	5	1
1	5	3	8	9	2	7	4	6
7	4	2	1	6	5	9	3	8
9	1	7	2	5	4	8	6	3
5	8	6	3	1	9	4	7	2
3	2	4	7	8	6	1	9	5

46

6	4	9	1	2	7	3	8	5
3	2	8	5	4	9	6	7	1
5	7	1	6	3	8	2	9	4
2	3	6	9	8	1	5	4	7
1	8	5	3	7	4	9	6	2
4	9	7	2	5	6	8	1	3
7	6	3	8	1	5	4	2	9
8	1	2	4	9	3	7	5	6
9	5	4	7	6	2	1	3	8

Solutions

47

9	3	5	8	7	1	6	2	4
6	7	4	2	9	3	5	1	8
1	2	8	5	4	6	7	9	3
4	1	2	3	6	9	8	5	7
7	6	3	1	5	8	9	4	2
8	5	9	4	2	7	1	3	6
3	8	7	9	1	2	4	6	5
2	4	1	6	8	5	3	7	9
5	9	6	7	3	4	2	8	1

48

7	8	3	9	2	6	1	5	4
1	5	4	7	8	3	2	9	6
6	9	2	5	4	1	3	7	8
2	3	5	8	1	4	7	6	9
8	7	1	3	6	9	4	2	5
9	4	6	2	7	5	8	1	3
5	1	8	6	3	2	9	4	7
3	2	9	4	5	7	6	8	1
4	6	7	1	9	8	5	3	2

Solutions

49

1	6	3	7	4	5	9	2	8
8	9	4	1	3	2	5	6	7
2	5	7	9	6	8	3	4	1
4	8	2	6	9	7	1	3	5
5	3	1	2	8	4	7	9	6
6	7	9	5	1	3	4	8	2
7	4	8	3	2	1	6	5	9
9	2	5	4	7	6	8	1	3
3	1	6	8	5	9	2	7	4

50

4	9	2	6	8	3	1	7	5
7	8	3	4	1	5	6	9	2
1	5	6	7	2	9	4	3	8
6	2	7	8	5	1	9	4	3
9	4	1	3	6	2	8	5	7
8	3	5	9	4	7	2	6	1
2	6	4	5	7	8	3	1	9
3	7	8	1	9	4	5	2	6
5	1	9	2	3	6	7	8	4

Solutions

51

7	3	9	4	6	5	2	1	8
6	2	8	7	1	9	4	5	3
4	1	5	3	2	8	7	9	6
3	6	7	5	8	2	1	4	9
2	9	1	6	7	4	8	3	5
5	8	4	9	3	1	6	2	7
9	7	2	1	5	6	3	8	4
8	4	3	2	9	7	5	6	1
1	5	6	8	4	3	9	7	2

52

6	1	8	3	5	2	9	4	7
7	9	3	6	1	4	5	2	8
4	2	5	7	9	8	6	3	1
9	7	2	5	6	3	1	8	4
1	5	6	8	4	7	2	9	3
8	3	4	1	2	9	7	6	5
5	6	9	4	3	1	8	7	2
3	8	1	2	7	6	4	5	9
2	4	7	9	8	5	3	1	6

Solutions

53

8	7	6	5	9	2	3	4	1
1	9	4	8	3	6	7	2	5
3	5	2	7	1	4	9	8	6
4	8	7	9	2	5	6	1	3
5	6	9	3	4	1	2	7	8
2	3	1	6	7	8	4	5	9
7	4	8	1	6	3	5	9	2
9	1	3	2	5	7	8	6	4
6	2	5	4	8	9	1	3	7

54

7	8	9	6	4	1	3	5	2
1	4	6	5	2	3	8	7	9
5	2	3	7	9	8	1	6	4
8	1	5	9	7	2	4	3	6
6	3	4	1	8	5	9	2	7
2	9	7	4	3	6	5	8	1
3	7	8	2	1	4	6	9	5
9	5	1	8	6	7	2	4	3
4	6	2	3	5	9	7	1	8

55

5	6	2	4	3	1	9	8	7
3	9	7	8	5	2	4	1	6
1	8	4	6	7	9	5	2	3
6	7	3	2	1	4	8	5	9
2	5	1	9	8	7	6	3	4
8	4	9	3	6	5	2	7	1
7	1	6	5	4	8	3	9	2
9	3	5	7	2	6	1	4	8
4	2	8	1	9	3	7	6	5

56

8	7	5	3	1	9	6	4	2
3	9	2	4	5	6	8	7	1
6	4	1	8	7	2	9	3	5
1	8	7	6	2	4	5	9	3
2	3	4	7	9	5	1	8	6
5	6	9	1	8	3	7	2	4
7	1	3	2	6	8	4	5	9
9	2	8	5	4	1	3	6	7
4	5	6	9	3	7	2	1	8

Solutions

6	1	5	9	3	4	8	2	7
7	3	2	6	8	1	4	9	5
8	9	4	5	7	2	3	1	6
1	4	6	7	9	3	2	5	8
3	8	9	2	5	6	7	4	1
5	2	7	4	1	8	6	3	9
4	6	1	8	2	5	9	7	3
9	5	8	3	4	7	1	6	2
2	7	3	1	6	9	5	8	4

1	6	8	3	9	4	5	2	7
7	3	4	1	2	5	9	8	6
5	9	2	8	7	6	4	1	3
9	1	5	6	8	3	7	4	2
3	2	7	5	4	9	1	6	8
8	4	6	7	1	2	3	5	9
4	5	3	9	6	8	2	7	1
2	8	1	4	3	7	6	9	5
6	7	9	2	5	1	8	3	4

Solutions

59

1	3	6	2	8	5	4	7	9
8	9	2	4	7	6	3	5	1
4	5	7	1	9	3	6	2	8
3	1	8	5	6	4	7	9	2
2	7	5	9	3	1	8	4	6
9	6	4	8	2	7	5	1	3
6	8	1	7	4	9	2	3	5
5	4	3	6	1	2	9	8	7
7	2	9	3	5	8	1	6	4

60

2	9	8	3	6	7	5	1	4
5	6	4	8	9	1	7	3	2
3	7	1	4	2	5	6	9	8
1	2	6	7	4	3	9	8	5
7	4	5	2	8	9	3	6	1
9	8	3	1	5	6	4	2	7
8	3	7	6	1	4	2	5	9
4	5	2	9	3	8	1	7	6
6	1	9	5	7	2	8	4	3

Solutions

61

8	3	6	1	5	4	7	9	2
2	7	5	6	8	9	1	4	3
4	9	1	2	3	7	8	5	6
3	8	2	4	6	1	9	7	5
5	4	9	7	2	3	6	1	8
1	6	7	8	9	5	2	3	4
7	2	3	9	4	8	5	6	1
9	5	8	3	1	6	4	2	7
6	1	4	5	7	2	3	8	9

62

1	4	7	8	3	5	9	6	2
6	8	2	1	9	4	5	7	3
5	3	9	7	6	2	4	8	1
3	2	8	9	5	1	7	4	6
9	7	6	4	8	3	2	1	5
4	5	1	6	2	7	3	9	8
7	9	3	2	1	8	6	5	4
8	6	5	3	4	9	1	2	7
2	1	4	5	7	6	8	3	9

63

5	8	3	2	7	9	4	6	1
4	2	1	5	8	6	3	7	9
6	7	9	4	1	3	8	5	2
8	3	6	9	4	2	5	1	7
1	4	5	6	3	7	2	9	8
7	9	2	1	5	8	6	3	4
3	6	7	8	9	4	1	2	5
9	5	4	3	2	1	7	8	6
2	1	8	7	6	5	9	4	3

64

9	3	5	4	6	1	2	8	7
7	8	2	3	5	9	1	4	6
6	1	4	2	7	8	9	5	3
4	9	3	5	2	7	6	1	8
1	6	7	9	8	4	5	3	2
5	2	8	6	1	3	7	9	4
3	4	6	7	9	5	8	2	1
8	7	9	1	4	2	3	6	5
2	5	1	8	3	6	4	7	9

Solutions

65

5	4	1	6	8	3	2	9	7
6	9	7	4	1	2	3	5	8
3	2	8	7	9	5	6	4	1
7	6	3	8	5	1	4	2	9
1	8	4	9	2	6	5	7	3
9	5	2	3	7	4	1	8	6
8	3	5	2	6	9	7	1	4
2	7	6	1	4	8	9	3	5
4	1	9	5	3	7	8	6	2

66

9	3	8	6	7	1	4	5	2
4	7	5	2	9	8	3	6	1
2	6	1	4	5	3	8	7	9
6	9	3	5	2	7	1	4	8
1	2	7	9	8	4	6	3	5
5	8	4	3	1	6	9	2	7
7	1	6	8	3	2	5	9	4
3	5	2	1	4	9	7	8	6
8	4	9	7	6	5	2	1	3

Solutions

67

6	1	5	7	3	4	9	2	8
2	8	4	9	6	1	7	5	3
3	7	9	8	5	2	6	1	4
4	5	6	3	2	7	1	8	9
1	2	7	6	8	9	4	3	5
8	9	3	4	1	5	2	6	7
9	3	2	5	7	6	8	4	1
7	6	8	1	4	3	5	9	2
5	4	1	2	9	8	3	7	6

68

4	3	7	6	5	8	1	9	2
8	9	6	7	2	1	3	5	4
1	5	2	9	4	3	7	8	6
3	8	5	1	6	7	4	2	9
2	1	9	4	3	5	8	6	7
7	6	4	2	8	9	5	3	1
6	7	3	8	9	4	2	1	5
5	2	1	3	7	6	9	4	8
9	4	8	5	1	2	6	7	3

Solutions

69

3	8	6	1	4	7	2	5	9
4	7	5	2	3	9	1	8	6
9	2	1	6	5	8	7	3	4
1	6	2	9	8	4	5	7	3
8	3	7	5	1	6	9	4	2
5	9	4	7	2	3	8	6	1
2	1	8	4	6	5	3	9	7
6	5	9	3	7	1	4	2	8
7	4	3	8	9	2	6	1	5

70

9	8	1	6	2	7	3	5	4
4	3	5	9	1	8	6	2	7
7	6	2	3	4	5	9	8	1
5	1	8	4	7	9	2	6	3
3	4	6	1	8	2	5	7	9
2	9	7	5	6	3	1	4	8
1	2	3	7	5	4	8	9	6
8	7	9	2	3	6	4	1	5
6	5	4	8	9	1	7	3	2

Solutions

71

2	8	7	1	6	5	9	4	3
9	1	5	8	3	4	6	7	2
6	4	3	9	2	7	5	8	1
1	7	8	3	9	6	2	5	4
4	2	6	5	8	1	7	3	9
5	3	9	7	4	2	1	6	8
3	5	2	6	1	8	4	9	7
7	9	4	2	5	3	8	1	6
8	6	1	4	7	9	3	2	5

72

9	3	4	7	6	5	2	1	8
6	2	5	3	1	8	7	9	4
8	7	1	9	2	4	5	6	3
4	1	7	8	5	2	9	3	6
2	5	9	1	3	6	8	4	7
3	6	8	4	9	7	1	5	2
7	8	3	5	4	1	6	2	9
5	9	6	2	8	3	4	7	1
1	4	2	6	7	9	3	8	5

Solutions

73

9	2	7	8	3	6	5	1	4
8	4	3	9	5	1	6	7	2
1	5	6	4	7	2	9	8	3
6	1	5	7	9	3	4	2	8
3	7	9	2	8	4	1	6	5
2	8	4	6	1	5	3	9	7
5	6	8	1	4	7	2	3	9
7	3	1	5	2	9	8	4	6
4	9	2	3	6	8	7	5	1

74

5	7	8	1	3	4	2	6	9
3	9	6	7	5	2	4	8	1
2	1	4	9	8	6	5	3	7
1	2	9	4	7	3	8	5	6
4	3	7	5	6	8	9	1	2
8	6	5	2	1	9	3	7	4
7	4	3	8	9	1	6	2	5
9	8	1	6	2	5	7	4	3
6	5	2	3	4	7	1	9	8

75

7	3	2	6	1	5	4	8	9
8	1	5	2	9	4	6	3	7
9	6	4	7	8	3	5	1	2
5	4	1	9	7	2	8	6	3
3	8	7	5	6	1	9	2	4
2	9	6	4	3	8	7	5	1
1	2	9	8	4	6	3	7	5
6	7	3	1	5	9	2	4	8
4	5	8	3	2	7	1	9	6

76

8	2	6	4	3	1	9	7	5
7	5	4	9	6	8	3	1	2
3	1	9	5	7	2	4	8	6
2	8	7	6	5	3	1	9	4
4	3	5	8	1	9	6	2	7
9	6	1	2	4	7	5	3	8
6	9	2	3	8	4	7	5	1
1	4	3	7	2	5	8	6	9
5	7	8	1	9	6	2	4	3

Solutions

77

5	1	4	7	8	9	3	2	6
6	2	3	5	1	4	8	7	9
9	7	8	6	3	2	1	5	4
4	3	9	1	6	5	2	8	7
1	6	7	3	2	8	9	4	5
2	8	5	9	4	7	6	1	3
7	4	6	2	9	1	5	3	8
3	5	1	8	7	6	4	9	2
8	9	2	4	5	3	7	6	1

78

8	5	6	2	3	4	7	9	1
1	7	2	6	8	9	5	4	3
3	4	9	1	7	5	6	8	2
4	2	8	9	6	7	3	1	5
7	6	5	4	1	3	8	2	9
9	3	1	5	2	8	4	7	6
6	1	3	7	4	2	9	5	8
5	8	4	3	9	1	2	6	7
2	9	7	8	5	6	1	3	4

9	5	7	4	6	3	1	2	8
3	4	8	1	9	2	5	7	6
6	1	2	5	8	7	9	3	4
4	6	3	9	1	5	7	8	2
5	2	1	7	4	8	6	9	3
7	8	9	2	3	6	4	1	5
2	7	4	8	5	9	3	6	1
8	3	5	6	7	1	2	4	9
1	9	6	3	2	4	8	5	7

9	8	7	3	1	6	2	5	4
2	4	5	8	7	9	3	1	6
6	1	3	5	2	4	9	8	7
5	7	1	6	8	2	4	3	9
8	6	2	4	9	3	5	7	1
4	3	9	1	5	7	8	6	2
7	9	6	2	3	5	1	4	8
3	2	8	7	4	1	6	9	5
1	5	4	9	6	8	7	2	3

Solutions

81

8	1	2	7	4	5	3	6	9
5	4	6	3	8	9	1	2	7
3	9	7	1	6	2	5	8	4
7	3	1	5	9	8	6	4	2
4	6	9	2	7	1	8	3	5
2	5	8	6	3	4	9	7	1
1	8	3	9	2	7	4	5	6
6	7	5	4	1	3	2	9	8
9	2	4	8	5	6	7	1	3

82

4	2	3	1	6	8	5	9	7
6	1	8	7	5	9	4	3	2
5	7	9	2	4	3	8	1	6
9	8	6	3	7	5	2	4	1
2	5	4	9	1	6	7	8	3
1	3	7	4	8	2	9	6	5
3	9	5	6	2	4	1	7	8
7	4	2	8	3	1	6	5	9
8	6	1	5	9	7	3	2	4

83

9	5	7	4	3	2	8	1	6
2	6	4	1	5	8	7	9	3
3	1	8	6	9	7	4	5	2
6	8	2	3	7	5	9	4	1
1	9	5	8	4	6	2	3	7
4	7	3	2	1	9	5	6	8
5	3	6	7	2	4	1	8	9
8	2	9	5	6	1	3	7	4
7	4	1	9	8	3	6	2	5

84

6	3	9	4	2	7	8	1	5
5	2	1	6	3	8	4	7	9
4	8	7	5	9	1	3	2	6
3	9	5	2	8	4	1	6	7
7	1	6	9	5	3	2	4	8
8	4	2	7	1	6	5	9	3
1	5	4	8	7	9	6	3	2
9	6	8	3	4	2	7	5	1
2	7	3	1	6	5	9	8	4

Solutions

4	7	5	2	1	3	9	8	6
8	2	1	4	9	6	5	3	7
9	6	3	8	5	7	1	2	4
5	1	4	3	8	2	6	7	9
2	3	7	9	6	4	8	5	1
6	9	8	5	7	1	2	4	3
3	8	9	1	4	5	7	6	2
7	5	2	6	3	9	4	1	8
1	4	6	7	2	8	3	9	5

8	2	1	3	6	7	9	5	4
3	6	4	8	9	5	1	7	2
5	9	7	2	4	1	3	6	8
2	5	8	4	1	9	7	3	6
9	4	6	5	7	3	2	8	1
7	1	3	6	2	8	5	4	9
1	3	2	7	8	6	4	9	5
4	8	5	9	3	2	6	1	7
6	7	9	1	5	4	8	2	3

Solutions

5	7	1	4	2	9	6	3	8
6	8	4	5	7	3	9	2	1
9	3	2	8	6	1	7	4	5
3	5	7	2	9	6	1	8	4
1	9	8	3	5	4	2	6	7
2	4	6	7	1	8	5	9	3
8	1	9	6	3	5	4	7	2
7	6	3	1	4	2	8	5	9
4	2	5	9	8	7	3	1	6

7	6	9	2	5	3	4	8	1
1	5	3	4	9	8	6	7	2
4	2	8	7	1	6	3	9	5
8	3	5	1	7	4	9	2	6
6	4	7	8	2	9	5	1	3
2	9	1	3	6	5	8	4	7
3	8	2	5	4	7	1	6	9
5	1	6	9	8	2	7	3	4
9	7	4	6	3	1	2	5	8

Solutions

4	5	2	1	7	6	3	8	9
6	9	3	5	4	8	2	7	1
1	7	8	3	9	2	4	5	6
8	1	5	9	3	4	6	2	7
9	6	7	2	8	5	1	3	4
2	3	4	7	6	1	5	9	8
7	4	9	6	2	3	8	1	5
3	8	1	4	5	7	9	6	2
5	2	6	8	1	9	7	4	3

3	8	5	4	1	7	6	9	2
7	4	6	3	9	2	5	8	1
9	1	2	6	8	5	7	3	4
5	7	3	9	6	1	2	4	8
6	2	1	7	4	8	3	5	9
8	9	4	5	2	3	1	6	7
4	6	7	2	5	9	8	1	3
2	5	8	1	3	4	9	7	6
1	3	9	8	7	6	4	2	5

91

1	9	2	5	3	6	7	8	4
5	7	3	9	4	8	2	1	6
6	8	4	7	2	1	3	9	5
9	5	1	6	7	2	4	3	8
7	2	6	3	8	4	9	5	1
4	3	8	1	5	9	6	2	7
3	4	5	2	1	7	8	6	9
2	6	7	8	9	5	1	4	3
8	1	9	4	6	3	5	7	2

92

8	3	4	5	1	7	6	2	9
2	7	6	9	4	8	5	1	3
1	9	5	2	6	3	7	4	8
3	4	8	6	7	1	9	5	2
9	5	7	4	8	2	1	3	6
6	2	1	3	5	9	8	7	4
4	6	3	1	9	5	2	8	7
7	1	2	8	3	6	4	9	5
5	8	9	7	2	4	3	6	1

Solutions

93

4	8	1	2	3	6	5	7	9
9	3	5	1	4	7	2	6	8
7	2	6	5	8	9	4	1	3
3	9	8	6	1	4	7	5	2
2	5	4	9	7	8	1	3	6
6	1	7	3	2	5	8	9	4
5	7	3	8	9	2	6	4	1
8	6	9	4	5	1	3	2	7
1	4	2	7	6	3	9	8	5

94

6	5	3	9	4	1	8	7	2
9	4	8	3	2	7	5	6	1
7	1	2	5	8	6	4	3	9
1	6	7	8	3	4	9	2	5
3	2	4	6	9	5	1	8	7
8	9	5	7	1	2	3	4	6
4	3	6	2	5	9	7	1	8
5	7	1	4	6	8	2	9	3
2	8	9	1	7	3	6	5	4

Solutions

95

2	4	9	7	5	6	8	1	3
1	5	6	2	8	3	7	9	4
3	7	8	9	1	4	2	6	5
9	6	1	8	7	5	3	4	2
7	8	2	3	4	1	9	5	6
4	3	5	6	2	9	1	8	7
5	9	3	1	6	7	4	2	8
6	2	7	4	9	8	5	3	1
8	1	4	5	3	2	6	7	9

96

7	8	5	3	2	6	9	4	1
2	1	3	7	4	9	6	8	5
4	6	9	1	5	8	3	2	7
6	5	1	4	7	2	8	9	3
9	4	8	6	1	3	5	7	2
3	7	2	9	8	5	1	6	4
5	9	6	2	3	7	4	1	8
8	2	4	5	6	1	7	3	9
1	3	7	8	9	4	2	5	6

Solutions

97

8	1	5	7	4	2	6	3	9
2	4	6	8	9	3	1	5	7
3	9	7	1	6	5	4	2	8
6	7	9	3	5	1	2	8	4
4	8	1	6	2	7	5	9	3
5	2	3	4	8	9	7	6	1
1	3	2	5	7	8	9	4	6
7	5	4	9	3	6	8	1	2
9	6	8	2	1	4	3	7	5

98

9	8	4	6	3	1	2	5	7
2	1	3	8	5	7	6	4	9
7	6	5	9	4	2	3	8	1
8	5	1	3	6	9	7	2	4
3	2	7	1	8	4	5	9	6
4	9	6	2	7	5	1	3	8
5	4	8	7	2	6	9	1	3
1	7	2	4	9	3	8	6	5
6	3	9	5	1	8	4	7	2

99

9	2	6	7	8	1	3	4	5
7	4	1	5	3	9	8	2	6
3	8	5	2	6	4	7	1	9
8	3	7	4	1	5	9	6	2
1	6	4	9	2	3	5	7	8
5	9	2	6	7	8	1	3	4
2	7	3	8	5	6	4	9	1
4	1	8	3	9	2	6	5	7
6	5	9	1	4	7	2	8	3

100

5	1	6	3	2	9	8	7	4
4	3	7	5	1	8	9	2	6
9	8	2	6	4	7	3	1	5
8	2	3	4	5	1	6	9	7
7	4	1	8	9	6	5	3	2
6	5	9	7	3	2	1	4	8
2	7	5	9	8	3	4	6	1
3	6	4	1	7	5	2	8	9
1	9	8	2	6	4	7	5	3

Solutions

101

2	4	6	5	8	3	9	7	1
8	1	5	4	9	7	3	6	2
3	7	9	6	1	2	8	5	4
4	5	1	9	6	8	2	3	7
6	2	8	3	7	1	4	9	5
7	9	3	2	4	5	1	8	6
1	8	4	7	5	9	6	2	3
9	3	7	1	2	6	5	4	8
5	6	2	8	3	4	7	1	9

102

5	8	2	4	7	6	1	9	3
6	3	7	8	1	9	5	2	4
4	9	1	3	5	2	8	7	6
3	7	5	1	9	8	6	4	2
8	2	6	5	4	3	7	1	9
9	1	4	6	2	7	3	5	8
7	5	8	9	6	4	2	3	1
1	4	3	2	8	5	9	6	7
2	6	9	7	3	1	4	8	5

103

3	1	4	6	7	2	8	5	9
5	2	8	4	3	9	6	1	7
6	9	7	5	8	1	3	4	2
2	7	6	1	4	8	9	3	5
9	3	1	7	5	6	4	2	8
4	8	5	2	9	3	1	7	6
8	4	3	9	2	7	5	6	1
7	6	9	3	1	5	2	8	4
1	5	2	8	6	4	7	9	3

104

7	3	1	9	6	4	8	5	2
4	9	2	3	5	8	1	6	7
6	8	5	2	7	1	4	3	9
2	6	7	5	4	3	9	1	8
3	5	8	7	1	9	2	4	6
1	4	9	6	8	2	3	7	5
9	7	4	8	3	6	5	2	1
8	1	6	4	2	5	7	9	3
5	2	3	1	9	7	6	8	4

Solutions

105

8	9	4	2	7	6	5	3	1
5	2	3	1	8	4	6	9	7
6	1	7	3	5	9	4	8	2
9	8	5	6	4	1	7	2	3
4	3	6	7	9	2	8	1	5
2	7	1	5	3	8	9	6	4
7	4	8	9	1	3	2	5	6
1	6	9	4	2	5	3	7	8
3	5	2	8	6	7	1	4	9

106

1	2	5	8	7	3	4	6	9
8	7	9	2	4	6	5	3	1
6	4	3	5	1	9	2	8	7
2	5	4	1	6	7	8	9	3
3	9	1	4	2	8	6	7	5
7	6	8	9	3	5	1	4	2
4	1	7	3	8	2	9	5	6
9	8	6	7	5	1	3	2	4
5	3	2	6	9	4	7	1	8

Solutions

107

8	2	3	7	5	6	9	4	1
7	5	6	4	1	9	3	2	8
1	9	4	3	2	8	7	6	5
3	4	7	9	6	1	5	8	2
2	1	9	8	3	5	6	7	4
5	6	8	2	7	4	1	9	3
9	8	5	6	4	3	2	1	7
6	7	1	5	8	2	4	3	9
4	3	2	1	9	7	8	5	6

108

7	6	1	9	3	2	5	4	8
5	9	3	4	6	8	2	1	7
2	8	4	1	5	7	6	3	9
6	5	9	3	2	1	7	8	4
1	4	7	8	9	5	3	2	6
8	3	2	7	4	6	1	9	5
3	2	5	6	8	9	4	7	1
4	1	8	5	7	3	9	6	2
9	7	6	2	1	4	8	5	3

Solutions

109

8	1	6	4	3	7	9	5	2
5	3	2	1	6	9	8	4	7
4	9	7	8	2	5	6	1	3
1	7	8	9	5	3	4	2	6
6	2	4	7	1	8	5	3	9
3	5	9	2	4	6	7	8	1
9	8	3	5	7	2	1	6	4
7	6	1	3	8	4	2	9	5
2	4	5	6	9	1	3	7	8

110

1	2	3	8	9	4	5	6	7
7	6	8	2	1	5	4	3	9
9	4	5	7	3	6	8	2	1
5	1	7	9	4	2	3	8	6
8	3	6	5	7	1	2	9	4
4	9	2	6	8	3	1	7	5
3	8	4	1	6	7	9	5	2
2	7	9	4	5	8	6	1	3
6	5	1	3	2	9	7	4	8

Solutions

111

7	8	3	6	1	4	9	2	5
2	4	1	9	3	5	6	7	8
9	6	5	7	2	8	4	1	3
3	7	9	5	4	2	1	8	6
5	2	4	8	6	1	3	9	7
8	1	6	3	9	7	2	5	4
4	5	2	1	7	3	8	6	9
6	3	7	2	8	9	5	4	1
1	9	8	4	5	6	7	3	2

112

6	4	2	9	1	7	5	8	3
3	7	5	8	6	4	2	9	1
9	8	1	3	2	5	6	4	7
4	2	8	1	9	3	7	6	5
5	9	7	2	4	6	1	3	8
1	3	6	7	5	8	4	2	9
7	1	3	4	8	2	9	5	6
2	5	9	6	3	1	8	7	4
8	6	4	5	7	9	3	1	2

Solutions

113

5	9	3	6	2	4	1	8	7
4	8	6	7	3	1	2	5	9
1	7	2	5	8	9	4	3	6
9	5	7	1	6	2	3	4	8
6	4	8	9	5	3	7	2	1
2	3	1	4	7	8	9	6	5
3	6	4	8	9	7	5	1	2
7	2	5	3	1	6	8	9	4
8	1	9	2	4	5	6	7	3

114

5	8	4	2	6	3	7	9	1
6	2	3	9	7	1	8	4	5
9	1	7	4	8	5	6	3	2
2	4	6	8	3	7	1	5	9
8	3	1	6	5	9	4	2	7
7	9	5	1	2	4	3	6	8
1	7	2	3	9	6	5	8	4
3	5	8	7	4	2	9	1	6
4	6	9	5	1	8	2	7	3

115

7	6	1	5	8	4	9	2	3
5	4	9	1	3	2	8	6	7
8	3	2	6	7	9	5	1	4
3	7	6	8	5	1	2	4	9
4	1	8	2	9	3	7	5	6
2	9	5	7	4	6	1	3	8
1	8	3	4	2	7	6	9	5
9	2	7	3	6	5	4	8	1
6	5	4	9	1	8	3	7	2

116

5	8	1	2	3	7	6	4	9
4	9	6	8	5	1	7	3	2
2	7	3	4	6	9	8	1	5
8	6	5	3	9	2	4	7	1
1	2	4	5	7	6	3	9	8
7	3	9	1	4	8	2	5	6
9	1	8	7	2	4	5	6	3
6	5	7	9	8	3	1	2	4
3	4	2	6	1	5	9	8	7

Solutions

117

8	7	3	6	1	5	4	9	2
4	1	9	3	8	2	6	7	5
6	5	2	9	4	7	8	3	1
3	6	1	7	9	4	5	2	8
5	9	4	8	2	1	7	6	3
2	8	7	5	6	3	1	4	9
9	4	6	2	5	8	3	1	7
7	2	5	1	3	6	9	8	4
1	3	8	4	7	9	2	5	6

118

7	5	3	9	8	6	4	1	2
4	9	1	3	7	2	8	5	6
6	2	8	1	5	4	9	7	3
3	6	9	7	4	1	5	2	8
1	4	7	5	2	8	6	3	9
2	8	5	6	3	9	7	4	1
5	1	4	8	6	3	2	9	7
9	7	6	2	1	5	3	8	4
8	3	2	4	9	7	1	6	5

Solutions

119

5	2	4	1	8	9	7	3	6
9	1	6	5	7	3	2	4	8
7	3	8	4	6	2	5	9	1
8	5	1	3	2	4	6	7	9
6	4	3	8	9	7	1	5	2
2	9	7	6	1	5	4	8	3
4	8	5	2	3	1	9	6	7
3	7	2	9	5	6	8	1	4
1	6	9	7	4	8	3	2	5

120

6	9	8	3	2	7	1	4	5
1	3	2	6	4	5	9	7	8
4	7	5	1	8	9	3	6	2
7	5	4	9	3	6	8	2	1
3	1	6	8	7	2	4	5	9
2	8	9	4	5	1	7	3	6
9	4	1	2	6	3	5	8	7
8	2	7	5	1	4	6	9	3
5	6	3	7	9	8	2	1	4

Solutions

121

1	4	6	7	5	8	2	9	3
7	2	5	3	9	1	8	6	4
8	9	3	6	4	2	7	5	1
9	8	4	2	1	5	6	3	7
6	1	2	9	3	7	4	8	5
5	3	7	8	6	4	9	1	2
2	5	1	4	8	6	3	7	9
4	6	9	1	7	3	5	2	8
3	7	8	5	2	9	1	4	6

122

4	5	8	3	1	2	9	7	6
6	2	9	4	5	7	3	1	8
3	7	1	6	9	8	5	2	4
9	4	7	8	6	1	2	5	3
8	1	2	9	3	5	6	4	7
5	3	6	2	7	4	8	9	1
7	6	3	5	4	9	1	8	2
1	8	5	7	2	6	4	3	9
2	9	4	1	8	3	7	6	5

123

8	5	7	2	9	1	6	4	3
6	2	9	7	3	4	1	5	8
3	4	1	8	6	5	9	7	2
9	6	5	1	8	2	7	3	4
2	7	4	6	5	3	8	9	1
1	3	8	9	4	7	2	6	5
7	8	3	4	1	9	5	2	6
5	9	6	3	2	8	4	1	7
4	1	2	5	7	6	3	8	9

124

2	5	8	7	4	6	1	3	9
4	9	6	8	3	1	2	7	5
3	1	7	2	5	9	4	6	8
9	6	5	4	8	2	7	1	3
1	7	4	9	6	3	5	8	2
8	2	3	1	7	5	9	4	6
7	3	1	5	9	8	6	2	4
5	8	2	6	1	4	3	9	7
6	4	9	3	2	7	8	5	1

Solutions

125

5	6	3	9	4	8	2	1	7
2	8	9	1	3	7	4	6	5
7	1	4	6	5	2	9	8	3
9	2	6	5	7	3	1	4	8
4	5	8	2	9	1	3	7	6
1	3	7	8	6	4	5	2	9
3	4	2	7	8	9	6	5	1
6	7	1	3	2	5	8	9	4
8	9	5	4	1	6	7	3	2

126

3	2	1	5	4	7	9	6	8
4	9	6	8	3	1	5	2	7
7	5	8	9	6	2	4	1	3
9	1	3	2	5	6	8	7	4
5	8	2	3	7	4	1	9	6
6	7	4	1	8	9	2	3	5
2	3	7	4	9	8	6	5	1
1	4	5	6	2	3	7	8	9
8	6	9	7	1	5	3	4	2

127

4	7	2	8	3	5	1	6	9
1	5	6	9	2	7	4	3	8
9	8	3	4	6	1	5	2	7
2	3	4	7	9	6	8	5	1
8	9	7	1	5	2	3	4	6
6	1	5	3	8	4	9	7	2
3	4	8	2	7	9	6	1	5
5	2	9	6	1	3	7	8	4
7	6	1	5	4	8	2	9	3

128

7	6	4	5	9	2	3	1	8
9	2	1	4	3	8	7	6	5
8	5	3	7	1	6	4	2	9
1	3	7	9	4	5	2	8	6
6	9	2	3	8	1	5	4	7
5	4	8	6	2	7	9	3	1
4	1	9	8	5	3	6	7	2
2	7	5	1	6	4	8	9	3
3	8	6	2	7	9	1	5	4

Solutions

129

3	6	4	7	1	5	8	2	9
2	1	8	3	4	9	6	5	7
5	7	9	2	8	6	4	1	3
7	8	5	4	9	3	2	6	1
6	9	2	5	7	1	3	8	4
1	4	3	8	6	2	7	9	5
8	5	1	6	3	4	9	7	2
9	3	6	1	2	7	5	4	8
4	2	7	9	5	8	1	3	6

130

3	5	4	6	2	8	1	7	9
9	2	1	5	3	7	8	4	6
8	6	7	1	4	9	3	5	2
7	8	9	3	1	5	6	2	4
6	1	2	7	8	4	5	9	3
4	3	5	9	6	2	7	1	8
2	7	6	8	9	1	4	3	5
1	4	3	2	5	6	9	8	7
5	9	8	4	7	3	2	6	1

131

6	2	8	9	1	5	3	4	7
7	4	1	8	3	2	6	5	9
9	3	5	4	6	7	1	2	8
1	8	9	6	4	3	2	7	5
4	7	3	5	2	8	9	6	1
2	5	6	1	7	9	4	8	3
8	9	4	3	5	6	7	1	2
3	6	7	2	8	1	5	9	4
5	1	2	7	9	4	8	3	6

132

6	1	8	3	4	2	7	5	9
7	3	2	8	5	9	4	1	6
5	4	9	1	7	6	3	8	2
1	8	3	6	2	5	9	7	4
9	6	5	7	3	4	1	2	8
4	2	7	9	8	1	5	6	3
2	9	1	5	6	3	8	4	7
3	7	4	2	1	8	6	9	5
8	5	6	4	9	7	2	3	1

Solutions

133

4	9	8	2	3	6	1	5	7
1	5	2	9	4	7	3	6	8
6	7	3	5	1	8	9	2	4
3	2	1	6	5	4	7	8	9
8	4	5	1	7	9	6	3	2
9	6	7	3	8	2	4	1	5
7	3	4	8	6	5	2	9	1
5	1	9	7	2	3	8	4	6
2	8	6	4	9	1	5	7	3

134

2	6	9	5	1	7	3	4	8
5	8	1	6	3	4	7	2	9
4	3	7	9	2	8	1	5	6
1	5	3	8	7	9	4	6	2
9	4	8	1	6	2	5	7	3
6	7	2	4	5	3	9	8	1
3	2	5	7	8	1	6	9	4
8	9	6	3	4	5	2	1	7
7	1	4	2	9	6	8	3	5

135

2	3	8	5	9	4	1	6	7
6	9	1	8	3	7	2	4	5
4	5	7	6	1	2	8	9	3
8	1	9	3	4	5	7	2	6
7	4	2	1	6	9	3	5	8
5	6	3	7	2	8	4	1	9
3	7	4	9	5	1	6	8	2
9	2	6	4	8	3	5	7	1
1	8	5	2	7	6	9	3	4

136

5	1	6	2	8	9	4	7	3
9	2	8	7	3	4	5	1	6
3	7	4	6	5	1	8	9	2
6	3	2	9	7	8	1	5	4
8	4	1	5	2	3	7	6	9
7	9	5	4	1	6	3	2	8
2	8	3	1	9	5	6	4	7
4	5	7	3	6	2	9	8	1
1	6	9	8	4	7	2	3	5

Solutions

137

4	1	5	9	7	2	8	3	6
9	2	7	3	6	8	4	5	1
8	6	3	5	4	1	9	7	2
6	3	1	4	9	5	2	8	7
7	9	2	1	8	6	5	4	3
5	4	8	2	3	7	6	1	9
1	8	9	6	5	3	7	2	4
3	5	6	7	2	4	1	9	8
2	7	4	8	1	9	3	6	5

138

5	3	8	7	6	1	4	9	2
7	4	1	9	3	2	5	6	8
2	6	9	4	8	5	1	3	7
3	5	2	6	1	7	8	4	9
9	8	4	5	2	3	6	7	1
6	1	7	8	9	4	3	2	5
8	9	3	2	5	6	7	1	4
1	7	5	3	4	9	2	8	6
4	2	6	1	7	8	9	5	3

139

8	1	2	9	3	5	7	6	4
3	7	9	2	6	4	5	8	1
4	5	6	8	7	1	2	3	9
1	9	4	6	2	3	8	5	7
6	2	7	4	5	8	9	1	3
5	3	8	7	1	9	6	4	2
9	4	3	5	8	2	1	7	6
2	6	5	1	4	7	3	9	8
7	8	1	3	9	6	4	2	5

140

4	2	3	7	8	9	1	6	5
5	1	9	3	6	4	2	7	8
7	8	6	1	2	5	4	9	3
8	5	1	6	4	7	9	3	2
6	4	7	9	3	2	5	8	1
9	3	2	5	1	8	6	4	7
2	6	8	4	7	1	3	5	9
3	7	5	2	9	6	8	1	4
1	9	4	8	5	3	7	2	6

Solutions

141

9	1	3	8	2	5	6	7	4
8	5	4	6	1	7	3	9	2
7	6	2	9	4	3	8	5	1
4	9	6	2	7	8	1	3	5
2	8	1	3	5	9	4	6	7
5	3	7	1	6	4	2	8	9
3	4	5	7	8	2	9	1	6
1	2	9	5	3	6	7	4	8
6	7	8	4	9	1	5	2	3

142

6	2	5	7	3	4	9	8	1
8	3	4	5	1	9	7	6	2
1	7	9	8	6	2	4	5	3
7	8	2	1	9	5	6	3	4
3	9	1	2	4	6	5	7	8
4	5	6	3	8	7	2	1	9
9	6	3	4	7	8	1	2	5
2	1	7	9	5	3	8	4	6
5	4	8	6	2	1	3	9	7

143

2	5	4	6	8	3	1	7	9
3	1	6	7	5	9	4	2	8
7	9	8	2	4	1	3	5	6
1	8	3	4	7	2	9	6	5
6	2	7	1	9	5	8	4	3
5	4	9	3	6	8	7	1	2
4	3	5	9	2	7	6	8	1
9	6	2	8	1	4	5	3	7
8	7	1	5	3	6	2	9	4

144

7	8	2	4	3	6	1	5	9
3	6	1	8	9	5	7	4	2
5	4	9	7	2	1	6	3	8
9	7	5	3	1	8	4	2	6
4	3	6	2	7	9	5	8	1
1	2	8	5	6	4	9	7	3
8	1	4	6	5	2	3	9	7
2	9	7	1	4	3	8	6	5
6	5	3	9	8	7	2	1	4

Solutions

145

4	9	3	2	1	8	7	5	6
1	5	6	4	7	9	3	2	8
7	8	2	5	3	6	9	4	1
3	2	4	1	9	5	6	8	7
6	7	9	8	4	2	5	1	3
8	1	5	3	6	7	2	9	4
2	3	7	9	8	4	1	6	5
5	4	1	6	2	3	8	7	9
9	6	8	7	5	1	4	3	2

146

6	3	7	9	5	1	2	4	8
1	2	5	8	6	4	9	7	3
4	8	9	2	7	3	1	5	6
7	5	6	1	8	2	4	3	9
8	9	2	4	3	6	7	1	5
3	1	4	7	9	5	8	6	2
5	7	8	3	1	9	6	2	4
2	6	1	5	4	8	3	9	7
9	4	3	6	2	7	5	8	1

Solutions

147

1	8	2	9	6	3	4	7	5
6	3	7	5	2	4	9	8	1
9	4	5	8	7	1	3	6	2
5	6	8	1	3	2	7	9	4
3	2	1	4	9	7	6	5	8
7	9	4	6	5	8	2	1	3
2	7	6	3	1	5	8	4	9
8	1	3	7	4	9	5	2	6
4	5	9	2	8	6	1	3	7

148

8	6	5	7	9	4	2	1	3
9	4	1	5	2	3	6	8	7
3	7	2	6	8	1	5	9	4
7	5	3	9	1	6	8	4	2
1	8	4	2	5	7	9	3	6
6	2	9	4	3	8	1	7	5
4	3	8	1	6	2	7	5	9
2	9	7	8	4	5	3	6	1
5	1	6	3	7	9	4	2	8

Solutions

149

1	6	3	9	7	4	2	8	5
2	8	7	1	3	5	4	9	6
9	4	5	6	2	8	1	7	3
4	2	1	3	9	7	6	5	8
6	5	9	8	1	2	7	3	4
7	3	8	5	4	6	9	1	2
8	9	2	7	6	3	5	4	1
3	1	6	4	5	9	8	2	7
5	7	4	2	8	1	3	6	9

150

1	5	4	2	9	8	7	6	3
6	8	9	5	7	3	1	4	2
3	7	2	6	1	4	8	9	5
4	9	8	1	5	2	3	7	6
2	6	7	3	8	9	4	5	1
5	1	3	7	4	6	9	2	8
9	3	6	4	2	1	5	8	7
7	4	1	8	6	5	2	3	9
8	2	5	9	3	7	6	1	4

Solutions

151

9	3	6	5	1	7	8	2	4
5	4	7	3	2	8	1	9	6
2	1	8	4	6	9	3	7	5
3	7	4	6	5	2	9	8	1
6	5	2	9	8	1	7	4	3
8	9	1	7	4	3	5	6	2
4	2	3	8	9	5	6	1	7
7	6	9	1	3	4	2	5	8
1	8	5	2	7	6	4	3	9

152

2	9	7	4	3	5	6	8	1
8	5	3	9	1	6	4	2	7
1	4	6	7	8	2	9	3	5
6	2	5	8	4	9	1	7	3
4	3	1	2	5	7	8	6	9
9	7	8	3	6	1	2	5	4
5	1	4	6	7	8	3	9	2
3	6	9	5	2	4	7	1	8
7	8	2	1	9	3	5	4	6

Solutions

4	3	2	6	7	5	1	8	9
5	1	8	4	9	2	6	3	7
7	6	9	3	8	1	5	2	4
2	4	7	8	1	3	9	6	5
9	5	1	2	4	6	8	7	3
3	8	6	9	5	7	2	4	1
6	9	3	5	2	4	7	1	8
1	2	5	7	3	8	4	9	6
8	7	4	1	6	9	3	5	2

9	2	5	8	6	7	4	3	1
7	4	8	9	3	1	2	5	6
3	1	6	4	2	5	7	9	8
1	6	2	5	8	4	9	7	3
5	7	4	3	9	6	8	1	2
8	3	9	7	1	2	6	4	5
6	8	3	1	7	9	5	2	4
4	9	1	2	5	8	3	6	7
2	5	7	6	4	3	1	8	9

Solutions

155

6	5	8	3	7	2	1	9	4
2	3	7	4	1	9	6	5	8
9	4	1	5	6	8	3	2	7
5	6	2	8	9	4	7	3	1
3	1	4	6	5	7	9	8	2
8	7	9	2	3	1	5	4	6
7	8	3	1	2	5	4	6	9
4	9	5	7	8	6	2	1	3
1	2	6	9	4	3	8	7	5

156

4	3	9	7	2	6	8	1	5
6	7	2	5	1	8	3	4	9
5	1	8	3	9	4	7	6	2
9	6	4	8	3	2	5	7	1
1	5	3	9	4	7	2	8	6
2	8	7	6	5	1	4	9	3
7	4	1	2	6	5	9	3	8
3	2	6	4	8	9	1	5	7
8	9	5	1	7	3	6	2	4

Solutions

157

3	1	4	8	6	9	5	2	7
5	7	8	1	4	2	3	6	9
6	2	9	5	3	7	4	8	1
7	5	3	2	1	6	8	9	4
8	6	1	7	9	4	2	5	3
4	9	2	3	8	5	7	1	6
1	4	7	9	2	8	6	3	5
9	8	5	6	7	3	1	4	2
2	3	6	4	5	1	9	7	8

158

4	7	3	2	9	1	8	6	5
9	2	1	8	5	6	4	7	3
6	5	8	3	4	7	9	2	1
5	3	7	4	2	8	1	9	6
1	8	9	7	6	5	3	4	2
2	4	6	1	3	9	7	5	8
7	6	2	9	8	3	5	1	4
8	1	4	5	7	2	6	3	9
3	9	5	6	1	4	2	8	7

6	2	8	7	9	1	5	3	4
5	1	9	4	8	3	7	2	6
3	4	7	6	5	2	8	1	9
1	8	3	2	6	9	4	7	5
9	5	4	8	3	7	1	6	2
7	6	2	1	4	5	9	8	3
2	9	1	3	7	4	6	5	8
8	7	5	9	2	6	3	4	1
4	3	6	5	1	8	2	9	7

4	3	9	7	8	1	6	2	5
1	7	2	5	3	6	4	8	9
6	8	5	4	2	9	3	7	1
5	2	4	9	1	3	8	6	7
8	9	1	6	7	4	5	3	2
3	6	7	8	5	2	1	9	4
7	5	3	1	9	8	2	4	6
2	1	6	3	4	7	9	5	8
9	4	8	2	6	5	7	1	3

Solutions

161

9	3	2	1	7	4	6	5	8
5	4	1	9	6	8	2	7	3
8	7	6	3	2	5	1	4	9
7	5	9	6	4	1	8	3	2
2	8	3	7	5	9	4	1	6
6	1	4	8	3	2	5	9	7
3	9	5	2	1	6	7	8	4
4	2	7	5	8	3	9	6	1
1	6	8	4	9	7	3	2	5

162

8	6	3	4	5	7	2	9	1
5	1	2	9	8	6	3	4	7
9	4	7	2	3	1	8	5	6
2	7	6	5	4	9	1	3	8
3	5	1	8	6	2	4	7	9
4	9	8	7	1	3	6	2	5
1	3	5	6	9	4	7	8	2
7	8	4	1	2	5	9	6	3
6	2	9	3	7	8	5	1	4

163

9	2	8	6	5	4	1	3	7
4	1	3	2	9	7	5	8	6
7	6	5	8	1	3	2	9	4
3	9	4	7	6	1	8	2	5
8	5	1	3	4	2	7	6	9
2	7	6	9	8	5	4	1	3
5	8	7	1	3	6	9	4	2
1	3	2	4	7	9	6	5	8
6	4	9	5	2	8	3	7	1

164

1	6	4	9	3	8	2	7	5
8	3	5	2	4	7	1	9	6
7	2	9	5	1	6	8	3	4
5	4	2	6	9	3	7	1	8
6	1	7	4	8	2	3	5	9
3	9	8	7	5	1	6	4	2
4	8	3	1	6	5	9	2	7
9	7	6	3	2	4	5	8	1
2	5	1	8	7	9	4	6	3

Solutions

165

9	4	3	2	1	8	7	5	6
5	2	6	3	7	9	1	8	4
1	8	7	6	4	5	3	9	2
7	6	1	9	3	4	8	2	5
4	5	8	7	2	6	9	1	3
2	3	9	5	8	1	4	6	7
3	9	5	8	6	7	2	4	1
6	7	4	1	9	2	5	3	8
8	1	2	4	5	3	6	7	9

166

4	9	5	7	6	3	8	2	1
1	6	8	4	2	5	9	3	7
3	2	7	8	9	1	4	5	6
2	1	6	3	5	9	7	8	4
5	3	4	1	8	7	2	6	9
7	8	9	6	4	2	3	1	5
8	5	1	9	3	4	6	7	2
9	7	3	2	1	6	5	4	8
6	4	2	5	7	8	1	9	3

167

2	9	8	4	1	6	7	3	5
4	5	3	8	2	7	6	9	1
6	1	7	9	5	3	2	4	8
3	6	9	1	7	8	5	2	4
1	4	2	6	9	5	8	7	3
8	7	5	3	4	2	1	6	9
5	3	1	2	6	9	4	8	7
7	8	6	5	3	4	9	1	2
9	2	4	7	8	1	3	5	6

168

9	5	2	8	7	4	1	3	6
1	4	6	3	9	5	7	2	8
3	7	8	1	2	6	9	5	4
6	8	5	9	4	1	2	7	3
7	1	3	2	5	8	6	4	9
4	2	9	6	3	7	8	1	5
2	6	4	5	1	9	3	8	7
8	3	7	4	6	2	5	9	1
5	9	1	7	8	3	4	6	2

Solutions

169

5	6	2	7	1	8	4	3	9
7	4	1	3	9	6	5	2	8
3	9	8	5	4	2	1	6	7
6	1	7	4	3	9	8	5	2
4	8	3	6	2	5	9	7	1
9	2	5	1	8	7	6	4	3
8	3	4	2	5	1	7	9	6
1	5	6	9	7	3	2	8	4
2	7	9	8	6	4	3	1	5

170

1	2	7	8	5	4	6	3	9
4	6	3	9	2	1	8	7	5
8	9	5	6	7	3	4	1	2
7	8	2	1	6	9	5	4	3
6	3	1	5	4	8	9	2	7
5	4	9	7	3	2	1	6	8
2	7	8	4	9	6	3	5	1
9	5	4	3	1	7	2	8	6
3	1	6	2	8	5	7	9	4

Solutions

171

6	2	5	9	7	1	3	4	8
4	7	9	8	6	3	1	2	5
8	1	3	5	2	4	7	9	6
9	3	7	1	8	2	6	5	4
1	8	6	7	4	5	9	3	2
2	5	4	6	3	9	8	7	1
3	9	1	2	5	8	4	6	7
7	4	2	3	1	6	5	8	9
5	6	8	4	9	7	2	1	3

172

8	4	3	6	7	2	9	1	5
2	9	7	3	1	5	4	6	8
1	5	6	4	8	9	3	2	7
6	3	8	7	4	1	5	9	2
9	7	5	2	6	8	1	4	3
4	2	1	5	9	3	8	7	6
5	6	4	9	3	7	2	8	1
3	8	9	1	2	6	7	5	4
7	1	2	8	5	4	6	3	9

Solutions

173

3	8	7	6	4	1	5	9	2
9	1	2	3	5	7	8	4	6
5	6	4	2	8	9	1	7	3
8	9	1	7	2	3	4	6	5
7	5	3	9	6	4	2	8	1
2	4	6	8	1	5	7	3	9
4	2	8	5	9	6	3	1	7
1	3	9	4	7	2	6	5	8
6	7	5	1	3	8	9	2	4

174

1	7	2	9	4	6	8	5	3
4	6	3	8	5	2	9	1	7
8	9	5	1	3	7	6	4	2
7	8	1	4	6	9	3	2	5
2	4	6	5	1	3	7	9	8
3	5	9	7	2	8	4	6	1
9	1	8	2	7	4	5	3	6
5	3	7	6	9	1	2	8	4
6	2	4	3	8	5	1	7	9

Solutions

175

4	5	9	6	3	7	1	2	8
6	2	7	8	9	1	3	4	5
1	3	8	5	2	4	7	9	6
3	9	5	2	4	6	8	7	1
2	8	1	3	7	9	6	5	4
7	6	4	1	8	5	2	3	9
9	7	6	4	1	2	5	8	3
5	4	3	7	6	8	9	1	2
8	1	2	9	5	3	4	6	7

176

9	4	1	2	5	6	7	8	3
7	8	5	9	4	3	6	1	2
2	6	3	7	8	1	9	5	4
1	2	4	3	9	7	8	6	5
5	3	9	8	6	4	1	2	7
6	7	8	5	1	2	3	4	9
4	1	2	6	3	9	5	7	8
3	5	7	1	2	8	4	9	6
8	9	6	4	7	5	2	3	1

Solutions

9	6	4	1	8	2	7	5	3
5	8	2	9	7	3	6	1	4
3	1	7	6	5	4	8	9	2
8	3	1	4	2	5	9	7	6
7	5	6	8	3	9	2	4	1
2	4	9	7	6	1	3	8	5
6	9	5	3	4	7	1	2	8
4	7	8	2	1	6	5	3	9
1	2	3	5	9	8	4	6	7

1	4	3	5	8	6	9	7	2
7	6	2	4	9	3	1	5	8
9	5	8	1	7	2	4	3	6
2	3	9	6	4	7	8	1	5
5	7	6	8	2	1	3	4	9
4	8	1	3	5	9	6	2	7
8	2	7	9	1	4	5	6	3
3	1	5	7	6	8	2	9	4
6	9	4	2	3	5	7	8	1

Solutions

179

5	6	9	3	2	7	1	4	8
8	2	4	9	1	6	3	5	7
1	3	7	5	4	8	6	9	2
2	7	5	1	8	9	4	3	6
4	8	6	2	5	3	7	1	9
3	9	1	7	6	4	2	8	5
6	4	3	8	9	2	5	7	1
7	1	8	6	3	5	9	2	4
9	5	2	4	7	1	8	6	3

180

1	8	4	3	5	2	7	6	9
9	6	7	1	4	8	3	2	5
5	3	2	9	7	6	8	4	1
8	2	1	6	3	7	5	9	4
7	9	5	8	1	4	6	3	2
6	4	3	2	9	5	1	8	7
3	7	9	4	8	1	2	5	6
2	1	8	5	6	9	4	7	3
4	5	6	7	2	3	9	1	8

Solutions

181

9	4	3	2	7	1	8	6	5
7	1	6	5	3	8	2	9	4
5	2	8	4	6	9	1	7	3
2	9	4	1	5	7	3	8	6
3	8	5	9	4	6	7	1	2
1	6	7	3	8	2	5	4	9
4	7	2	6	1	3	9	5	8
8	5	9	7	2	4	6	3	1
6	3	1	8	9	5	4	2	7

182

8	7	6	2	9	5	1	4	3
1	5	2	4	6	3	9	8	7
9	4	3	1	7	8	6	5	2
3	8	4	5	2	6	7	1	9
5	9	7	3	1	4	8	2	6
6	2	1	9	8	7	5	3	4
4	6	8	7	5	2	3	9	1
2	1	5	6	3	9	4	7	8
7	3	9	8	4	1	2	6	5

Solutions

183

3	1	2	7	9	6	4	5	8
7	5	4	3	1	8	6	2	9
6	8	9	2	4	5	3	1	7
5	6	7	4	8	9	1	3	2
8	4	1	5	2	3	7	9	6
2	9	3	1	6	7	5	8	4
1	3	8	9	7	4	2	6	5
9	7	5	6	3	2	8	4	1
4	2	6	8	5	1	9	7	3

184

9	2	4	8	3	1	5	7	6
5	6	8	7	4	9	3	1	2
3	1	7	2	5	6	8	9	4
4	3	5	9	7	2	1	6	8
6	9	2	5	1	8	7	4	3
7	8	1	3	6	4	2	5	9
2	4	6	1	8	7	9	3	5
1	5	9	6	2	3	4	8	7
8	7	3	4	9	5	6	2	1

Solutions

185

1	2	5	8	6	7	9	4	3
6	4	8	2	3	9	1	7	5
7	9	3	1	5	4	2	8	6
8	6	1	5	4	3	7	2	9
3	5	2	9	7	1	8	6	4
4	7	9	6	8	2	3	5	1
2	1	7	4	9	6	5	3	8
9	8	6	3	2	5	4	1	7
5	3	4	7	1	8	6	9	2

186

8	6	1	2	7	3	9	4	5
5	2	9	4	8	6	3	7	1
4	7	3	1	9	5	8	6	2
7	8	6	3	2	9	1	5	4
9	1	5	6	4	8	7	2	3
2	3	4	7	5	1	6	8	9
1	5	2	8	3	7	4	9	6
3	9	8	5	6	4	2	1	7
6	4	7	9	1	2	5	3	8

Solutions

187

2	4	5	7	6	9	8	3	1
3	1	9	8	2	5	4	7	6
6	8	7	3	4	1	9	5	2
5	2	6	1	9	7	3	4	8
4	3	1	5	8	6	2	9	7
7	9	8	4	3	2	6	1	5
9	5	2	6	7	4	1	8	3
1	6	3	9	5	8	7	2	4
8	7	4	2	1	3	5	6	9

188

1	3	8	7	6	2	9	4	5
9	5	2	3	1	4	8	7	6
7	6	4	8	5	9	3	2	1
8	4	3	1	7	6	5	9	2
2	9	1	4	8	5	7	6	3
6	7	5	2	9	3	1	8	4
5	1	6	9	2	8	4	3	7
3	8	7	6	4	1	2	5	9
4	2	9	5	3	7	6	1	8

Solutions

189

2	5	6	9	8	3	4	7	1
9	3	8	4	1	7	2	6	5
7	4	1	2	5	6	3	9	8
1	9	4	3	6	5	7	8	2
8	6	7	1	2	9	5	4	3
5	2	3	7	4	8	9	1	6
3	1	5	6	7	4	8	2	9
6	7	9	8	3	2	1	5	4
4	8	2	5	9	1	6	3	7

190

1	9	4	5	7	6	8	3	2
5	6	8	9	2	3	7	4	1
2	3	7	8	1	4	5	9	6
7	4	2	6	9	8	3	1	5
6	5	9	2	3	1	4	7	8
8	1	3	4	5	7	6	2	9
3	8	1	7	6	9	2	5	4
4	7	5	1	8	2	9	6	3
9	2	6	3	4	5	1	8	7

Solutions

191

6	1	4	7	5	9	2	3	8
9	7	2	8	3	6	4	1	5
5	8	3	1	4	2	6	9	7
7	6	8	4	1	3	9	5	2
2	5	9	6	7	8	3	4	1
4	3	1	9	2	5	7	8	6
8	4	6	5	9	7	1	2	3
3	9	7	2	8	1	5	6	4
1	2	5	3	6	4	8	7	9

192

4	8	7	9	1	3	6	5	2
1	6	2	5	8	4	7	3	9
5	3	9	7	6	2	4	1	8
3	2	8	1	7	5	9	4	6
6	7	1	2	4	9	3	8	5
9	4	5	6	3	8	2	7	1
2	5	3	8	9	7	1	6	4
8	1	4	3	2	6	5	9	7
7	9	6	4	5	1	8	2	3

Solutions

193

3	4	2	5	8	1	6	9	7
5	9	1	6	2	7	8	4	3
7	8	6	4	3	9	5	2	1
9	3	7	1	5	8	2	6	4
8	6	4	7	9	2	3	1	5
2	1	5	3	6	4	7	8	9
4	2	3	9	7	6	1	5	8
1	5	8	2	4	3	9	7	6
6	7	9	8	1	5	4	3	2

194

1	5	8	4	6	3	2	7	9
4	2	9	8	5	7	3	1	6
7	6	3	9	1	2	4	8	5
2	1	4	7	9	8	6	5	3
5	8	6	2	3	1	9	4	7
3	9	7	6	4	5	1	2	8
6	3	2	5	8	4	7	9	1
9	7	5	1	2	6	8	3	4
8	4	1	3	7	9	5	6	2

195

7	9	8	4	1	2	5	6	3
2	5	4	9	3	6	8	7	1
3	1	6	8	5	7	4	9	2
5	8	9	6	4	1	3	2	7
4	6	3	2	7	5	9	1	8
1	7	2	3	8	9	6	4	5
8	4	1	7	9	3	2	5	6
9	2	7	5	6	8	1	3	4
6	3	5	1	2	4	7	8	9

196

1	5	4	8	2	6	9	7	3
7	9	6	5	1	3	4	8	2
8	3	2	9	7	4	5	6	1
4	8	5	1	6	2	7	3	9
3	2	7	4	9	5	6	1	8
9	6	1	3	8	7	2	4	5
5	1	8	6	4	9	3	2	7
6	7	9	2	3	1	8	5	4
2	4	3	7	5	8	1	9	6

Solutions

8	5	3	4	9	2	7	6	1
1	4	6	3	5	7	9	2	8
9	2	7	6	8	1	4	5	3
6	8	9	7	1	3	5	4	2
4	1	5	8	2	6	3	9	7
7	3	2	9	4	5	1	8	6
3	6	8	5	7	4	2	1	9
2	7	4	1	6	9	8	3	5
5	9	1	2	3	8	6	7	4

9	8	6	2	4	7	3	5	1
2	5	3	9	8	1	7	6	4
4	7	1	6	3	5	2	8	9
6	9	7	5	2	3	4	1	8
1	4	8	7	6	9	5	2	3
5	3	2	8	1	4	6	9	7
8	1	5	4	7	6	9	3	2
3	6	4	1	9	2	8	7	5
7	2	9	3	5	8	1	4	6

Solutions

5	9	2	7	4	3	8	6	1
7	3	6	1	9	8	5	4	2
8	1	4	5	2	6	7	9	3
2	8	5	9	6	1	4	3	7
1	7	9	3	8	4	6	2	5
6	4	3	2	7	5	9	1	8
9	2	1	6	5	7	3	8	4
4	6	7	8	3	2	1	5	9
3	5	8	4	1	9	2	7	6

8	1	5	2	3	6	9	4	7
9	3	4	1	8	7	6	5	2
7	2	6	4	5	9	3	8	1
3	8	9	7	6	1	4	2	5
5	6	2	3	4	8	1	7	9
1	4	7	5	9	2	8	6	3
6	9	3	8	2	5	7	1	4
4	5	1	6	7	3	2	9	8
2	7	8	9	1	4	5	3	6

Solutions